BIKE PATH
RAPIST

To Oksana—
thanks for reading.

Jeff S___

BIKE PATH
RAPIST

A Cop's Firsthand Account of Catching the Killer
Who Terrorized a Community

JEFF SCHOBER

WITH

DETECTIVE DENNIS DELANO

The Lyons Press
Guilford, Connecticut
An imprint of The Globe Pequot Press

The Lyons Press is an imprint of The Globe Pequot Press.

Text designed by Libby Kingsbury

Library of Congress Cataloging-in-Publication Data

Schober, Jeff.
  Bike path rapist : a cop's firsthand account of catching the killer who
terrorized a community / Jeff Schober and Dennis Delano.
        p. cm.

  ISBN 978-1-59921-606-5

1. Sex crimes—Investigation—United States. 2. Serial murderers—
United States. I. Delano, Dennis. II. Title.

  HV8079.S48.S36 2009

  364.15′32092—dc22

                                        2008046743

Printed in the United States of America

10 9 8 7 6 5 4 3

CONTENTS

Foreword

When I was asked to work on the multi-agency investigative team now known as the "Bike Path Rapist Task Force," I could never have imagined the events that would transpire in the years ahead. On the first day, the higher-ups told us that we were not to use the words "task force" in our dealings with the media, because it had undesirable political connotations and might lead people to think a "metro police force" could be tried out in the area. It was decided that a team of investigators would be staffed from four separate local police jurisdictions including the Erie County Sheriff's Office, the New York State Police, the Town of Amherst police department, and the City of Buffalo police department. Along the way, more personnel from these four agencies were added as different investigative talents and skills became needed. When all was said and done, the task force had consisted of between five and twelve investigators at various times. Most people considered the task force a huge success, especially after the dust had settled and we had put the cuffs on the man Sheriff Tim Howard later called the "monster known as the Bike Path Rapist." The investigation led to the arrest, conviction, and sentencing on three separate counts of murder of Altemio

Sanchez, who was living what appeared to be a normal life as an average family man, factory worker, husband, and father of two in the Buffalo suburb of Cheektowaga, New York.

Ironically, the Cheektowaga police department, although they assisted us at various times during the investigation, had not been a part of the task force, because none of the crimes that we were commissioned to investigate had been committed within their jurisdiction. During the course of the investigation, I had done some research on what is called "geographical profiling," and was amazed at how accurately it could pinpoint the most likely areas where a serial criminal might reside, work, and commit crimes. As the saying goes, if given an option, an animal usually will not soil his own cage. I later found out that it is uncommon for serial killers and rapists to commit crimes in their hometowns.

The investigation culminated with an arrest that should have been the pinnacle of my career in law enforcement, but was partly overshadowed by a struggle between cops trying to do the right thing and an out of control district attorney trying to protect his turf.

I cannot begin to imagine the pain and suffering that this monster has caused countless victims and family members during his reign of terror, nor will I ever forget the emotional women as they wept while trying to discuss the crimes. I also won't forget the feeling of helplessness we had because we would never be able to charge him with the twenty-six rapes of mostly teenaged girls that we believe he had committed, because the statute of limitations had expired.

Along the way, through this twisted and jumbled investigation, we stumbled upon the heartbreaking realization that a young diagnosed schizophrenic named Anthony Capozzi had been wrongfully arrested and convicted for two rapes he could not have committed and had served twenty-two years out of a thirty-five-year sentence. These crimes were later proven by DNA to be the work of none other than the Bike Path Rapist. As if this wasn't strange enough, the Erie County district attorney and his staff were adamant that they were not going to pursue the information that we had uncovered about Capozzi unless we could give them "hard physical evidence" that he did not commit the rapes in question. The first question that popped into my head was "Why?" Why do we need "hard physical evidence" that Anthony did not commit the rapes in order to get him released from prison, when there was absolutely no physical evidence, hard or otherwise, linking him to any crime scene anywhere back in 1985 when he was arrested, tried, and convicted?

My heart goes out to the Capozzi family for their never-ending support for Anthony, and the tight bond that they have maintained throughout this unconscionable ordeal. They have held their heads high, knowing that some day the truth would surface. I am both humbled by their humanity and compassion for others, and grateful to God for being given the opportunity and ability to be involved in helping such a wonderful family to finally attain justice for their son and brother.

I have often said since then that this investigation could not have been resolved successfully, especially in such a short time, without the participation of every person who was involved with the task force. Good or bad, right or wrong, *everyone* served a purpose during the many months leading to the conviction of Altemio Sanchez and the release of Anthony Capozzi. There were many other investigators who did much more work than I did on these cases, but for one reason or another were not able to come forward and speak about them. I felt that I had no choice but to speak out publicly about the Bike Path Rapist case; I hoped to pressure the powers that be into taking a deeper look at some of the more obvious flaws in our legal system, flaws that allowed prosecutors to diddle around and play word games while a person's life hung in the balance.

The Bible says that "iron sharpens iron." I take that to mean that as long as dialogue is taking place between people, there is a good chance that the correct decisions will eventually be made, and the truth will surface from it, no matter how long it has been suppressed. I believe that is what transpired in this case.

—*Detective Dennis Delano*
Cheektowaga, NY

INTRODUCTION

The Detective, the Case, and the City

In a seventy-year-old precinct house at the intersection of Church and Franklin Streets in the guts of downtown Buffalo, a tiled room on the third floor is home to the Homicide/Cold Case Unit. Four detectives share its space, with one closet-sized office and another interview room large enough for two chairs and a computer. A dry-erase board fills an entire wall, where cases are charted in different colors to convey their status. Mug shots tacked to bulletin boards reveal sketches of killers both wanted and apprehended. Alongside the bad guys, photos of cops in trench coats stare with hardened features.

Here, a daily battle is waged between death and long-forgotten truth.

Detective Dennis Delano's desk is near the door. It is symbolic, perhaps, that his work zone is separate from his colleagues, because Delano is an independent thinker who is often frustrated by politics and the slow pace of bureaucracy.

At fifty-six, Delano is a big man, with an ample stomach, a wide neck, and fingers thick as rolled nickels.

A full head of dark hair, a rounded nose, and spreading jowls lend him an intimidating appearance. Listen to his gravelly voice and imagine a suspect melting beneath his glare.

He is a a man without pretensions, a quintessential "Buffalo guy." Delano does not care for self-importance or inflated egos. He has only one goal: Unearth the truths that time has blurred.

"A bit of an attitude," was how *Dateline NBC* described him. Many of his colleagues agree, comparing his rough demeanor to Andy Sipowicz from *NYPD Blue*. Some go further, suggesting the sign above a nearby aquarium—DOES NOT PLAY WELL WITH OTHERS—describes the man as much as the temperamental and eponymous fighting fish "Little Dennis."

There is one thing no one disputes. Delano is a first-rate cop.

"I deal with dead people and their families," Delano explained in muted tones. "You can't help but make it personal."

He was behind this desk on November 15, 2006, when the chief of detectives requested he join a team to hunt a long-standing serial killer. For more than twenty years, a nameless man dubbed the "Bike Path Rapist" had attacked, raped, and murdered women and girls in Western New York. After twelve years of silence, forensics had matched DNA from a recent crime scene to the killer everyone thought had disappeared. It was a request that would change lives.

In the course of the next several months, a team of exceptional officers from different law enforcement agencies collaborated to capture a serial killer who had run amok since the early 1980s. He turned out to be an ordinary man with a wife and two kids. With his arrest, a community reclaimed its peace of mind.

But Delano and his colleagues discovered something else along the way: An innocent man had been convicted and was serving time for rapes he did not commit. Anthony Capozzi, suffering from mental illness, had spent twenty-two years in prison. Detectives were convinced of his innocence, but could find no hard evidence to prove it.

"I had never come across a situation like this before," Delano explained. "We didn't know what to do to get this guy out. He was coming up for parole but they had denied him five times already and they were going to deny him again. I was waking up in the middle of the night knowing this guy was sleeping in a little cell, and he didn't belong there. It was unconscionable."

Justice was long delayed, but Delano did not give up. Encouraged by fellow task force members, who left daily notes urging him to "Free Capozzi," Delano's moral strength kept him focused. Through tenacity, justice prevailed. Because of Delano and his fellow investigators, a long-forgotten file was discovered containing DNA slides that proved the Bike Path Rapist had attacked the women Capozzi had been convicted of raping. Capozzi was released just before Easter 2007.

There have been big cases for Delano, both before and since, but this story is unlike any other.

"It's really the apex of my career," Delano said reflectively. "There's nothing else to compare it to."

Reminders are kept close by. A photo on Delano's bulletin board freezes one poignant moment that made all the setbacks worthwhile. Four women—the mother and three adult sisters of Anthony Capozzi—are locked in a jubilant hug only seconds after they learned Anthony had been exonerated.

When Delano was invited to join the task force, it was a logical progression in his diverse and successful career.

"There aren't a whole lot of accidents," Delano reflected, discussing the abilities of the men and women who worked together to capture the killer. "Our past experiences give us talents in certain areas. Life often leads you in a direction, and people with influence notice and steer you that way."

Becoming a cop was never Delano's career goal. In fact, as a young man, he had an aversion to police.

"Before I got married, I was a drummer in a hard rock band in the 1960s," Delano explained with a smile. "I wasn't too fond of cops back then. They would come in, break up our parties, and I used to throw things at them. I wanted nothing to do with cops."

Ironic, then, that Delano would become synonymous with the virtues of the Buffalo police. As a young man, he worked many different jobs. He built concrete walls, enlisted in the military at age seventeen, and married at eighteen. Always interested in firefighting and first aid, after the service he joined a volunteer fire company. He drove ambulances and went to paramedic school through Erie Community College. Delano was certified in New York State but couldn't get a job.

"There was a TV program called *Emergency* about a paramedic unit in Los Angeles. I knew they needed paramedics in California, so I went to the library, looked up addresses, and wrote letters to every town on the coast. I could challenge the exam there, but I needed a sponsor. One company agreed to sponsor me if I worked for them."

His wife had a job in Western New York as a nurse at the Veterans Administration Hospital, but she was willing to leave—jobs were easy to come by, especially in California. They held a garage sale and literally sold everything, then bought a van and drove to the West Coast. Their son had just been born and their daughter was seven.

Delano became a fireman-paramedic, assigned to the seedier part of Hollywood. After working there for a year, he had discovered two loves: the water and the weather. Otherwise, he hated California.

"I couldn't stand all the uppity people," Delano recalled. "The ones who weren't uppity were the surfer boys. They walked around calling everybody *dude*. Half the firemen I worked with owned surfboard repair shops."

It was a far cry from his native city. The fit between man and geography was out of synch. Absent the sincerity and blue-collar lifestyle he had experienced growing up in Buffalo, Delano's impatience flared.

The couple flew home for a family wedding and realized how much they missed living there. After spending time at their old hangouts, seeing friends, they dreaded going back to California. Within a month, everything was sold again. They bought a camper van and returned to Western New York.

"My brother was parks commissioner at the time and he told me the fire department was looking to expand," Delano recalled. "This was beautiful. I had experience no one else did, so I was sure to be hired. But they were only interested in adding minorities."

Another brother, Paul, was a homicide detective. He urged Dennis to consider law enforcement. Paul visited Dennis's house and talked about upcoming police exams. He even brought applications. Dennis was working for an aluminum siding business, but found it tedious during the depths of winter. He began taking different civil service tests. He applied for the state police, city police, and Erie County Medical Center security. Starting in 1980, he worked for three years at the county holding center as a sheriff's deputy, then three more years with the Buffalo Municipal Housing Authority in plainclothes, until he became a Buffalo cop in 1985.

Delano spent sixteen years in the Auto Theft Squad until it was abolished as part of a departmental reorganization. A unit was formed called Major Crimes, dealing with homicides, robberies, and assaults. After a few years, Buffalo's brass realized this was not the most efficient use of their detectives.

"It was almost impossible to investigate a homicide one minute and a bank robbery the next," Delano recalled. "That's when the department went back to a Homicide Unit and I transferred to it."

During his time in Major Crimes, Delano took it upon himself to learn the skills needed to become a top investigator.

"I didn't have a clue how to investigate a murder, and police training is scarce. I was left to figure things out on my own. Fortunately, I had a brother who had been an ace homicide guy before he retired. I asked him how to do things. He suggested going back and reading old files to see how guys solved cases in the past. That way I would learn the order to proceed."

Unfortunately, there was little organization to the homicide files. They were scattered in boxes throughout the building wherever there was extra space. Delano discovered folders slowly and began studying. His fascination grew. Using his own money, he bought textbooks and read about gathering details at investigation scenes. He used the Internet as a research tool.

"I always want to be the best at whatever I'm doing," Delano said.

So he asked everybody for advice. He trudged down to the building's basement, found old files, and blew the dust off cardboard box tops. His brother Paul pointed out interesting cases that were never solved, so he pulled them to have a look. All this was done on his own time, and he started getting better at it by training himself. He read a few files and thought, *This one could still be solved*. After he put a couple cases together, the bosses began to notice.

"Soon I was overwhelming myself with old cases. Then some funding came through so I dispersed a few to other guys. But when the money went dry, all the files ended up back on my desk." Delano laughed as he recalled the circular route of cold cases. "Then it was worse than before because I didn't know what other investigators did or didn't do."

Medical problems began to interfere with Delano's day-to-day life. He suffered from sleep apnea, frequently dozing at his desk. He took work home and completed it at odd hours, when rest was elusive. The man who had never used a sick day in more than twenty years was granted medical leave. He went from questioning suspects to undergoing stress tests. His health concerns grew, and in 2005, he considered retirement.

"I was denied Social Security benefits, or I would have," he said. "I'm glad now it worked out the way it did."

In May 2006, the Buffalo police formed a Cold Case Squad, with room for four full-time detectives. Because of his special interest in old files, Delano was invited to join. But after eight months away from the job, questions lingered about his wellness.

"I wanted to try," Delano admitted. "It seemed like a good use of my skills. I told the boss that if my health didn't hold up, I would just go back on medical leave. The first case I pulled was one from 1974 that I'd been working all along, and that was solved.[1] Shortly after that, the Bike Path case came up, and I said I'd love to be part of that."

---

[1] In 2008, Buffalo stagehand Leon "Rusty" Chatt was convicted for the murder of Barbara Lloyd.

Located on the eastern edge of Lake Erie, Buffalo evolved into a national trading center with the opening of the Erie Canal in 1825. Products from the Midwest passed through Buffalo en route to the Hudson River and New York City. By 1832, its population quadrupled, from 2,500 to 10,000. In a short time, it became the nation's premier inland port.

Prosperity continued steadily. At the beginning of the twentieth century, Buffalo's population made it the country's eighth largest city. Fifty years later, it was still the fifteenth largest American metropolis and a hub of industry and culture. But gradually the good times ebbed away. The Erie Canal lost its influence due to the opening of the St. Lawrence Seaway in 1957. The 1970s were not kind to the region. Steel mills closed, railroads lost their prominence, and pollution reigned. Buffalo became the embodiment of a rust belt city.

By 2005, years of steady population decline left Buffalo as the nation's forty-sixth largest city. A recent report ranked the urban core as the second poorest in the nation.

The community projects an inferiority complex; there is a palpable feeling in the air that better things must be happening elsewhere. This may be caused partly by the weather, which gets a bad rap, even though cities to the east like Rochester and Syracuse annually accumulate more snow. And then there are the long-term failures of its two major sports teams, football's Buffalo Bills and hockey's Buffalo Sabres. For four straight seasons, from 1991 to 1994, the Bills advanced to the Super Bowl, only to lose. (Cynics suggested Buffalo's area code be changed from 716 to 044.) In existence since 1970, the Sabres, likewise, have lost both times they advanced to the Stanley Cup finals. Still, people remain passionate about sports.

There are two sides to Buffalo. Summers feature moderate temperatures with low humidity. People in Western New York are largely unpretentious, down-to-earth. It maintains its reputation as a blue-collar community, although modern times feature a mix of industry, health care, and education. Wealthy pockets exist in certain city neighborhoods and the suburbs.

Traffic is manageable and the infrastructure is sufficient to handle the region's daily needs. A thriving arts community, an elaborate park system, and historic architecture are all boasting points.

It is within this community that a serial rapist lived, attacking women anonymously beginning in the 1970s.

Case History

No one is sure how the Bike Path Rapist eluded capture for more than twenty years. His attacks were scattered across Western New York, linked by common elements including morning assaults, use of a rope or wire garrote, comments made to each victim, and physical descriptions of the attacker.

When the task force formed in November 2006, the case was well known among police, the media, and even ordinary citizens. Since the 1980s, there had been several crimes attributed to the Bike Path Rapist:

- A forty-four-year-old woman was dragged from the exercise path around Delaware Park on Thursday, June 12, 1986. After raping her, the attacker tightened the ligature around her neck until she was rendered unconscious.

- A seventeen-year-old victim was raped along a wooded shortcut behind Frontier High School in Hamburg, a suburb south of the city, on Monday, July 14, 1986.

- A sixteen-year-old female was accosted near a train track in Buffalo's Riverside neighborhood and dragged to a nearby junkyard, where she was raped on Friday, June 10, 1988.

- Using the same path as the prior Riverside victim, a fifteen-year-old girl was raped near an abandoned building on Monday, May 1, 1989.

- On the morning of Thursday, August 24, 1989, a fourteen-year-old high school student walked to summer school along the Willow Ridge Bike Path in Amherst. She was seized with a ligature, lifted over a wire fence, and dragged to a clearing in a wooded area near the trail. She was raped and left unconscious after he tightened the garrote around her neck.

- A thirty-two-year-old businesswoman walked the Ellicott Creek Bike Path at 7:30 a.m. on Tuesday, May 31, 1990. Unlike the other victims, she did not see her attacker, but only felt a cord loop around her neck from behind. She was quickly rendered unconscious and raped. Although there was no semen sample, authorities believe the location, time of day, and method of assault link this to the Bike Path Rapist.

The next two rapes escalated to murder.

• Linda Yalem, a student at the University at Buffalo, was accosted just after noon on Saturday, September 29, 1990, along the Ellicott Creek Bike Path. After an intensive search, her partially clothed body was discovered off the path the following day.

• Majane Mazur was a thirty-two-year-old mother struggling with drug addiction and working as a prostitute when she went missing in October of 1992. Her half-naked body was discovered in a field along a railroad track near Exchange Street in one of Buffalo's more desolate industrial areas. It was not until 2004 that DNA test results connected this homicide to the Bike Path Rapist.

• On Wednesday, October 19, 1994, a fourteen-year-old girl was raped behind a junkyard off Military Road in Riverside.

Then, without explanation, the attacks stopped.

✳

Most surviving victims had seen the rapist well enough
for composite sketches to be created. He was, they agreed,
a white male with Mediterranean features, possibly Ital-
ian or Hispanic. He stood between 5'5" and 5'9", had dark
hair beneath a baseball cap, with a mustache and thick
eyebrows. He was thought to be between twenty-five
and forty years old. He generally wore exercise clothes:
sweatpants and jacket, a jogging suit, and sneakers. He
carried a fanny pack and sometimes used duct tape to
gag or blind his victims.

His most common method of attack was to pose as
a jogger. After spotting a lone female, he ran toward her
from the front while boldly staring into her eyes, then
averted his gaze as he passed. Once beyond the victim,
he acted quickly, pivoting and sprinting back to loop a
ligature around her neck. Securing control from behind,
he kept a tight stranglehold and moved to the front, sliding the knot around the windpipe, alternately choking
and releasing pressure to control consciousness. Survivors recall passing out within seconds as their throats
constricted. The victim would be dragged into a wooded
area, away from view. As she faded in and out of lucidity,
depending on the tightening or loosening of the garrote,
the rapist commanded her not to look at him, despite the
fact she had seen his approach. He often forced women
to cover their heads with a piece of clothing.

His signature was a "double ligature" indentation
on victims' necks. Some women still bear the scars after
more than two decades.

The attacker may have employed one long wire that
was looped twice, or had two ropes attached at either

end. "He didn't always get the cord over the victim's head cleanly," Delano explained. "Several women had rope burns on their cheeks and chin where he scraped when he tried to loop them from behind."

Attacks occurred primarily in the morning, the earliest being 7:30 a.m. and the latest just after noon. He pre-selected locations, not victims.

The attacks occurred between May and October. This was not a coincidence; during those months the foliage provided cover.

"I picture this guy like a little troll lurking in the brush waiting for a woman to come by," Delano said. "If the opportunity was right, he'd rape her. He had to stalk women at that time of year, because once leaves weren't on the trees, he'd have nowhere to hide."

It was puzzling that no third party saw the rapist before or after an assault. The fact that he remained anonymous for so long was extremely uncommon and one of the things that frustrated Delano the most. In a majority of cases, a witness sees a struggle or hears noises alerting them to a crime being committed. With these attacks, nobody but the rapist and the victim saw anything.

"Nobody saw this guy," Delano noted. "He was completely invisible, like a ghost. It's strange because he was not just in a location briefly for the rape, he was hanging around these areas beforehand, scouting things out, yet somehow remained undetected."

One woman may have watched the killer accost Linda Yalem. She contacted Amherst police a week after the 1990 murder. On that Saturday, she traveled along a highway overlooking the Ellicott Creek Bike Path. She reported a man in a yellow sweatshirt crossing a footbridge with his arm around a woman's neck, only yards from where Yalem's body was discovered. The witness, however, assumed the couple was engaged in horseplay, and she did not realize the event was suspicious until later.

How did the killer remain invisible? One conjecture was that he disguised himself in a park employee uniform. This could allow him to move along paths with a cloak of anonymity. If he had been spotted, no one would think twice about encountering a maintenance worker. But that contradicted reports by victims that he dressed in workout clothes, so the angle was abandoned.

Science helped narrow the search, but DNA analysis was in its infancy in the late 1980s and early 1990s. Results showed his genetic makeup was a mixture of European and Native American. Later tests also revealed that between 1992 and his last known attack in 1994, he lost the ability to produce sperm. This could have been caused by any number of factors, including testicular cancer or a vasectomy. While this information provided a clue, it did not pinpoint a predator.

Investigators were puzzled when the violence ceased after 1994. As months of silence stretched to years, theories abounded: The nameless man was imprisoned, had moved away, or was dead.

No jailhouse snitches came forward with information. No similar attacks or DNA matches were reported around the Western New York region or elsewhere in the country. Perhaps the Bike Path Rapist had taken his secret to the grave.

He might have, had he not resumed action after a dozen years. On the sixteenth anniversary of his first murder, the Bike Path Rapist struck again.

When he was in high school, his mother unveiled an awful truth. For years, its stark reality was too overwhelming to think about. When he did, anger rose inside him, like a slithering brown worm. In many ways, the revelation changed the way he viewed life.

He had been a mistake.

When he was born, there were three other children, all under the age of four. Signs of trouble were evident in his parents' marriage: Dad took solace in alcohol and other women, while Mom had her hands full trying to maintain the house and raise kids.

In Puerto Rico in the 1950s there were few options to terminate a pregnancy. But his mother was adamant that she did not want another baby. She secured a combination of pills, with the promise that if ingested, they would induce a miscarriage. She swallowed the drugs, but the intended effect never occurred. On January 19, 1958, her last child was born.

After his capture, decades later, he would wonder if the bad medicine had somehow been absorbed into his system, altering his genetic makeup. Were those pills a factor in the malevolent behavior? Was his condition inborn, because of choices his mother made during her pregnancy?

Learning this awful truth—he was not wanted—was devastating as a teenager. But his mother revisited the issue from time to time as he grew into adulthood. For the rest of his life, that burden weighed heavily on him. A few months before her death in 2005, she reiterated that his existence had been a mistake.

"Sometimes that triggers me, thinking what she said," he recalled placidly. "But I told her, I'm fine, Mother."

In spite of this millstone, he was a survivor. Until he met his wife, no one had wanted him. He had never been popular, never had many friends or girlfriends while growing up. Still he carved a niche for himself, marrying and raising two children of his own.

But he wasn't fine. That knowledge triggered something deep within, and a dark filament flared. It had been twelve years since he had done any bad things. Yet when his mother said that, he wanted to hurt women again.

Joan Diver

Indian summer signals an ending, a last burst of warmth before air dips colder and frost blankets the morning landscape. On Wednesday, September 20, 2006—a comfortable Indian summer night—Shelly Fuller* of Amherst wanted to savor such a day.[2] After dinner, Fuller walked the Ellicott Bike Path with her fourteen-pound cocker spaniel–poodle mix, Tully.

The Ellicott Bike Path is a paved five-mile trail that winds through Amherst. Adjacent to streams and woods, the path weaves across the campus of the University at Buffalo (UB).

Fuller was familiar with the bike path, often traveling there during the day, but her husband had a meeting that night and she knew opportunities to be outdoors were waning with autumn's approach. Scanning a bulletin board near the parking lot on North Forest and Maple Roads, Fuller saw a woman enter the path nearby. Fuller recognized the perils of using the trail by herself, and decided to stay close by the woman so neither would

---

[2] Events in this book are true, but where an * is inserted, a real name has been replaced with a pseudonym to ensure privacy.

be alone. As the dog sniffed the ground, Fuller detoured toward a September 11th monument and circled the site with Tully.

The sun was setting faster than she expected, and when Fuller looked around, she realized her unofficial walking companion had continued out of sight. Fuller backtracked along the path toward a narrow lane of blacktop with woods on both sides. Suddenly, Tully froze, eyes and ears alert, nose twitching at invisible scents. Facing left, with head held stationary, the dog emitted a low growl.

Perhaps it was a squirrel or rabbit in the woods, but Fuller thought she heard something larger moving through the brush. Could it be a deer? Thick foliage prevented her from seeing the source. Frightened by her dog's reaction, she moved off the path toward a ridgeline of trees near a gully.

"I heard what sounded like a person stepping in the wooded area behind me," Fuller said. "I looked up and down the path but I was completely alone."

She began to jog when she spotted a lifeline. An older man appeared on the trail ahead of her, near a footbridge. Although several hundred feet away, Fuller yelled and waved to get his attention, but he did not notice and soon disappeared from sight.

In the evening stillness, a rustling resumed behind her.

Approaching panic mode, Fuller thrust her hand into her pocket and brushed against her cell phone. She had forgotten it was there. With quivering fingers she used speed dial to call her husband, then remembered he was in a meeting and his phone would be off. As the stalking noise grew closer, Fuller pretended she was talking to someone nearby.

"I'm almost at the bridge," she said loudly into the phone. "Do you see me?"

Breaking into a sprint, with Tully in tow, she raced to the span and crossed, sweat beading her forehead.

Looking back, a man emerged from the woods on the other side of the stream. He bent down to retrieve something from the brush. Fuller's heartbeat pulsed, and she took off running again.

As she neared a clearing that opened onto North Forest Road, Fuller heard something approach behind her. The man from the woods was pedaling a mountain bike with straight handlebars, coming directly toward her. In his late forties or early fifties, he had deep-set brown eyes. His forehead was covered with a baseball cap, but his eyebrows were darker than the hair on the side of his head, and his round face scowled as he passed. He was athletic looking, wearing gray sweatpants, sneakers, and a green T-shirt over a long-sleeved white undershirt.

Fuller sensed relief as he went by, and quickly made her way toward the tennis courts. She felt safer within view of players volleying back and forth. She wondered where the man had hidden the bike, because she had not seen it before crossing the bridge.

But the biker was not through. He had turned around and was now riding toward Fuller once more, staring with a look of controlled rage. She had done something to upset him.

"He rode past me again, and gave an evil, smirking grin," Fuller recalled. "He looked mad as hell."

Fuller kept her eyes locked on his, meeting the gaze, trying to remember every detail about him. It was now too dusky to see distance, but fading from Fuller's sight, he rode slowly back toward the woods where she had first heard him prowling.

When Fuller reached her car, she sat down, locked the doors, and exhaled. Her adrenaline had been sky high, and was now slowly getting back to normal. She began to weep. There was something evil about the encounter. The man held a secret and she had stumbled upon it.

Fuller went home and doodled with a pad and pencil. She sketched a portrait of him, with strings of hair flowing from beneath the baseball cap. She added a dimple to his chin, and a thin line of mustache. Darkened circles provided shading around the eyes, but she admitted they were not accurate. The nose wasn't quite right either. She was not sure how to fix it.

Fuller remained upset that night. She remembered the story of the Bike Path Rapist, and went online to search out information about his attacks. Although he had been quiet since 1994, several past assaults had occurred along the trail she walked. Almost sixteen years earlier, University at Buffalo student Linda Yalem had been murdered near the spot Fuller had walked just hours before.

In the morning, she called the Amherst police and recounted her story. She requested that officers be alert at the bike path, because she sensed something bad might happen. Later that day, Fuller went to the station and dropped off her sketch.

The following Sunday, September 24, she and her husband walked up and down the path, stopping females who traveled alone. The couple recounted Fuller's story, warning anyone who would listen.

Five days later, just past the neighboring town of Clarence, Joan Diver was strangled and killed along a secluded bike path.

He led a double existence, but was unable to explain his behavior. He never told his wife, never confided in anyone. It was a burden he carried alone.

"I don't know what makes me be one person one time and the next something clicks in my head where I commit these crimes," he said.

Some of the anger was rooted in his boyhood, when he claimed to have been abused by his mother's boyfriend. By high school, those memories bubbled to the surface, and he considered seeking a counselor. But how do you confess such a thing, especially as a shy teenage boy? As he grew older, he wanted to share the story with his sister. But she was tough. She wouldn't want to face that; he knew she would take his mother's side. His mother had been aware of the abuse, but was too scared to say anything, and that angered him. What woman refused to defend her child? She was so afraid of her boyfriend, in fact, there was one night when she slept in the woods, staying out until dawn, shivering through darkness, until he left the house the following morning.

Anger and fantasy combined into a noxious flame, fueling his desire. The rapes were about control.

"It made it more exciting. It made me more over the top. That was a good feeling."

He is fuzzy about victims' names, although they have been recounted in the media and he has read the stories. Yet he remembers the locations where an attack occurred and what the girl was wearing.

"To me it's not rough sex, it's more about fantasy. My raping got worse where I couldn't control it at all. I never intended to kill them. But when she put up a fight, I wanted control, and I took it. I knew that once I killed one person I could do it again."

Pornography was not a turn-on. With a wife and two boys, he would never allow that into his house. An attack would happen when the urge became too great to suppress.

"I think what made me do it is something that's got to be up here," he reflected, tapping his head. "I can be one person one day and another person to commit these crimes. I wish I knew. When the urge comes, it's there, and I gotta do what I gotta do. Time goes by and I know I have to have sex with somebody and rough them up."

He cannot explain the long gap of inactivity between 1994 and 2006, other than to say that he knew it was imperative to stop. He sensed he was about to be caught.

"I was very, very scared. I had a talk with myself and stopped for twelve years."

Still, his sexual appetite remained voracious. He hired prostitutes from the city, as often as three times per week. He frequented a small stable of girls that he knew, but never harmed any of them. With condoms purchased at a supermarket on Grant and Amherst Streets in Buffalo, he would rendezvous with a hooker. Each encounter cost $40 or $50. The payments began to escalate as his frequency grew.

He cannot explain what made him resume in 2006.

"The more I was seeing prostitutes, the more the sexual drive was coming back to me. It was getting worse and worse. I couldn't control it. My philosophy was I needed to rape somebody again and take control. If I could explain it to you, I would. But it's hard for me to know even myself how I led these two separate lives."

Only two people knew for sure how events transpired on the Clarence Bike Path during the morning of September 29, 2006, and one killed the other.

A mother from Clarence was strangled with a wire garrote that day, leaving behind a husband and four children. In the aftermath of her body's discovery, the community questioned the safety of rural bike paths, while women were reminded to take precautions during outdoor workouts. Although there were no witnesses, the Bike Path Rapist left a single droplet of sweat on a steering wheel that proved he was involved in this crime. This revelation, six weeks after the murder, led to the formation of a task force whose sole purpose was to snare the predator.

Through interviews, forensics, and testimony from the killer, officers pieced together a snapshot of that fateful morning.

Joan Diver, a forty-five-year-old homemaker, dropped her son off at day care just before 9:00 a.m. Between then and 11:30, when he needed to be picked up, she planned to complete errands and jog along the trail that snaked through town.

Sometime within a window of two hours, Joan Diver parked her Ford Explorer in a paved lot at the foot of Salt Road. She ran east, crossing Davison Road. It is believed that she proceeded further to Barnum Road and reversed direction, backtracking toward her SUV, when she was assaulted on the return trip. Her sunglasses were knocked from her face when a garrote was forced over her head. The ligature scraped her left cheek. Her broken sunglasses were later discovered on the south side of the trail.

Although much of the area has dense foliage on either side of the blacktop, east of Davison Road there is a clearing where a gas pipeline crosses beneath the trail. Trees recede and the terrain dips into a gully on the north. From the bike path, the southern view opens onto a steep rising hill, beyond which, out of sight, is Main Street. The northward view faces the back of a poultry farm on Davison Road.

The killer dragged Joan Diver into the clearing approximately forty feet north, then some twenty feet east under a thick wooded canopy. Although only a few yards away, it is difficult to hear any noise from the bike path because of different elevations and thick foliage. During the struggle, the back of Diver's head struck a tree trunk or fallen log. The autopsy revealed a bruise on her skull.

Diver was left on her back, wearing running shoes on both feet, with spandex shorts pulled down and gathered around her left ankle. A blue sweat jacket was laid across her, stretching from the breastbone to just below her pubic area. Her iPod was discovered underneath the body, its cord tangled in a nearby branch, snagged there during the struggle when she was dragged from the path.

Curiously, she was not raped.

Clarence and Newstead are two rural suburbs east of Buffalo. An eight-mile bike path, formerly a railroad track, slices through the towns' dense wooded areas. The trail tilts along a southwest to northeast axis, roughly paralleling Main Street. It stretches behind Clarence High School on the southern side of Route 5, then crosses north at Salt Road and continues into Newstead.

"I did research on these old rails to trails," Delano said. "Nationwide they are a haven for rapists because they are usually isolated with thick foliage on either side."

Delano believes the killer planned his attack for September 29 along the Ellicott Creek Bike Path in Amherst, where his first murder occurred sixteen years before. But while scouting locations for a rape site on Wednesday, September 20, a fluke encounter with a woman and her dog interrupted that plan, so he sought an alternate spot.

"The back of Clarence High School lets out onto the bike path," Delano said. "Kids use that route on their way to school. It's my opinion that he was nearby scoping out young girls. When the bell rang and there were no more girls coming, he missed his chance."

The Bike Path Rapist had attacked teenagers before, on trails near Frontier High School in Hamburg and Sweet Home High School in Amherst, so the m.o. was already established. Specific women were not targeted—rather, the rapes were crimes of opportunity. He hid in the brush, and when a solitary girl appeared, he accosted her.

On September 29, 2006, however, there was no opportunity. The girls walking to school that morning traveled in groups, or those who walked alone remained within sight of someone else. Frustrated by circumstances, the killer traveled east, searching for a victim.

"He had a bicycle that day," Delano said. "He rode up the path toward Shisler Road and hid the bike in the woods. I believe he arrived at Salt Road when Joan Diver was getting out of her vehicle. He watched her start running and went halfway up the path, knowing she planned to come back, and grabbed her then. He had to do an attack that day, because it was the 29th, and he knew which vehicle belonged to her."

Many have tried to figure out how the killer ended up in Clarence and Newstead when his previous attacks had never been that far out. Delano is certain he was scared of being discovered in Amherst and found another spot. That was why he had that angry look in his eyes when he rode past Fuller on his bike. She had ruined everything.

After Joan Diver's murder, Fuller was deflated. She had seen the killer and reported him, providing a detailed description and even a sketch. Yet still a woman died. She felt that few had taken her warnings seriously. Had she done enough? She regretted not posting fliers at the entrances to every bike path in the area. If she had done so, would Joan Diver have seen the warning and had second thoughts about running alone? It was a question that haunted Fuller.

"I know it was God who protected me," she admitted in the days following Diver's death. "I saw this guy for a reason, and I hope it's to put him in jail for the rest of his life."

Once he recognized the perils of attempting an attack in Amherst, the rural trail through Clarence became the killer's second choice.

On September 29, a half-mile from the Salt Road parking lot, east of Davison Road, he lurked in the brush. No one had noticed him riding his bicycle, which was concealed nearby in tall weeds just off the paved path. He held a loop of wire in his hands, and his brain was jittery, as if it would burst.[3]

---

[3] The killer later insisted that he used a nylon rope, as he had in previous attacks, but forensic experts matched the imprints of wounds on Joan Diver's neck to the texture of malleable wire. A saleswoman at a local hardware store testified she sold the wire to the killer. He denied even knowing where that hardware store was located.

He had discovered the parking lot accidentally en route to a golf course. Adjacent to the trail, he pulled in, turned off the ignition and watched for a long time. It was nearly deserted; only a few people went up and down the path.

The next time he visited, he waited until he was alone, and took a few tentative steps onto the blacktop. Dark memories surged. Like an addict reintroduced to a drug, he felt an old pang of desire. For long stretches, the trail sliced through dense foliage, rural and secluded. There were so many perfect spots.

But it had been years. He had been a much younger man the last time, although he didn't recall exactly when that had occurred. Something made him stop, but even in his mind he had difficulty explaining why. Fear of being caught was part of it, the idea that those he loved would learn of his double life. It was morally wrong; he understood that. The women were innocent, simply random victims of his urges. He had been lucky enough to avoid capture back then, but technology had advanced rapidly in the intervening years. If he began again, could that luck continue?

If you do this, he thought to himself, *you're going to get caught*.

But the lure was too strong. Once he encountered this trail, he came back, three or four times each week for nearly a month. It was inevitable. Someone was going to be hurt again.

Now, lurking in the bushes, he noticed the woman approaching. She was slim, a white baseball cap covering her head, exposing only tips of blonde hair tied back. His pulse pounded faster, senses heightened. He remained still, frozen as if squeezed in a vise, until her footfalls pounded a few feet from him. He leaped out and bounded two strides.

Despite music piped from her earbuds, the woman heard his approach and turned suddenly, screaming as he forced the garrote over her head. She scratched at his face, catching a fleck of skin near his eye. She twitched and contorted, trying to evade the wire encircling her neck.

He felt as if stitches were popping in his brain. When she fought it made him angrier.

A Fatal Weekend

When Joan Diver disappeared, no one suspected the Bike Path Rapist was responsible. In fact, during the three days before Diver's body was discovered, she was officially considered a missing person, because there was no evidence of foul play or murder. Unlikely as it might have seemed, some wondered if she had simply fled the family without informing her husband. There had been no outward sign of marital troubles, but perhaps there was a compartment of her life that remained shielded from outsiders. Did domestic issues divide Steven and Joan Diver? Were there financial discrepancies? Might one of them be having an affair? Could the husband have killed her and hidden the body?

Such are standard police inquiries when a spouse vanishes. Questions were raised about the last hours of Joan's life and her husband's subsequent behavior. According to witnesses, evidence and police statements, there were no simple answers.

✳

Joan Diver and her husband Steven began Friday, September 29, with a typical suburban routine. There was always a morning rush to get the kids off to school, to ensure lunches were packed and bookbags stuffed with last night's homework. Steven, a chemistry professor at the University at Buffalo's Amherst campus, was due at the lab that day.

Despite the fast-paced morning, the couple made time for coffee, discussing plans for dinner that evening. Maybe they would see a movie afterward. Steven suggested they buy an electric toothbrush for their four children, ages fourteen, twelve, nine, and four. Saying goodbye to the family, he climbed into his Oldsmobile at 7:50 a.m.

Joan proceeded with her morning schedule. Trained as a critical care nurse, she had interrupted her career to raise children, but planned a return to work the following fall, when Carter entered kindergarten. Now, she valued this time away from a job, time that she could savor as a mother. At forty-five, she appeared ten years younger with blonde hair, a rounded face, and pale-colored eyes that gave way to an easy smile.

In addition to volunteering at the day care and with her kids' Boy and Girl Scout troops, being away from emergency rooms had allowed her freedom to pursue hobbies. She had become a fitness enthusiast, running twenty miles per week. Steven's university colleagues referred to her affectionately as a "faculty wife," a nickname bestowed upon a woman who manages home life, raises kids, and attends scholastic functions while her husband devotes himself to academics.

The couple met while attending classes at the University of Utah, according to relatives. Married since 1990, Joan and Steven had lived in Madison, Wisconsin, where he received his Ph.D., and Boston, Massachusetts, where Steven worked at Harvard, before moving to Western New York in 1997. By September 2006, Joan felt content. Their kids were doing well in school, she was physically fit, and had recently returned from visiting her native Utah. After nearly ten years in the area, she had settled into the rhythms of life around Buffalo.

When dropping her son at Village Daycare in the morning, it was not unusual for Joan Diver to be dressed in running clothes. She often donned spandex, a tank top, and white sneakers with lime green stripes before heading directly to the bike path for a run. When picking up her boy after class ended, Joan's blonde hair might be wet from a post-workout shower.

On September 29, Joan wore street clothes. She had a list of errands to complete, but had informed her husband that she planned to go running. She made some of the stops, then ventured home, changed into exercise gear, and wrapped a blue fleece sweatshirt around her waist. She would run the path and continue chores after she picked up Carter.

"The only person who knew she would be running that day was Steven," Delano said. "We know she wasn't stalked ahead of time because it was her first time exercising outside in a couple weeks."

Joan Diver parked her green Ford Explorer in a lot on Main and Salt Roads and left a full water bottle tucked into a dimple of the center console. Carrying only her keys, sunglasses, and an iPod, she took a deep breath, did a light stretch, and began to jog east along the blacktopped trail.

As she entered the trail from the parking lot, Joan passed a metal sign reminding women of the perils of running alone: BE SAFE—WALK WITH A FRIEND. Joan had spoken with her sister in Massachusetts about safety precautions, like varying her route along different paths, not becoming predictable. The family had even considered buying a dog to accompany her during regular runs. But this morning Joan was by herself.

Steven Diver arrived in the chemistry department at UB's Natural Sciences Complex at 8:20 a.m. and went to the third floor. A slight man, with gold-rimmed glasses and blonde hair spilling over his collar, the thirty-eight-year-old Diver had the pale skin of someone who spent long hours indoors. A detective later described his complexion as "pasty."

According to Diver's own account, that day he conducted an experiment inside a teaching lab, working alone. Beginning with the moment he left home that morning, there were large blocks of time during which no one could verify his whereabouts. Although this routine was his standard practice, on the day his wife was killed, his solitude left investigators wondering if Diver was involved, especially when witnesses testified to unusual behavior.

When Diver emerged from the lab at 10:45 a.m., for example, he bumped into a fellow professor who had just entered the complex. Encountering his colleague, Diver's face contorted.

"He was in an agitated state of mind," the man recalled. "His reaction to my presence was unlike anything I had seen in ten years of knowing him. Upon seeing me, his expression was one of surprise, then changed to anger or hatred and I felt threatened. The hairs on the back of my neck went up."

He backed into the hallway, asking Diver what was wrong.

"He returned to normal and said that everything was okay," the professor claimed. "Steve Diver has always been a straight arrow. This was so out of character and inconsistent with every action I have seen from him."

It was an incident that likely would have been forgotten under normal circumstances. But this was not to be a normal day.

After he spoke briefly with his co-worker, there was another seventy minutes of time in which Steven Diver was alone. Shortly before noon, a student came into his office and found him eating lunch at his desk.

Diver was respected for his academic work, but people at UB's chemistry department agree that he did not possess an outgoing personality. He was aloof, rarely interacting with graduate students. One Ph.D. student said, "Mr. Diver was the most unsociable person I have ever met. . . He doesn't take criticism well. He is probably the most intelligent organic chemist in our department and he'll have no problem reminding you of that if you question it."

A woman from Newstead was en route to a bank on Friday, September 29. After 10:00 a.m., while driving along Utley Road, she slowed almost to a stop at the bike path's intersection. Twenty feet away, emerging from the trail, a man slouched, limping and holding his right hand as if he were injured.

"There was a blank look on his face," the woman said. "He had sandy brown hair, a tan jacket, a white shirt with dark stripes, and light blue jeans. He had a strange facial expression that scared me, like you know you did something wrong, like you can't believe you did that. He looked like he was in a state of shock. I worked as a nurse and I've seen that expression before. He straightened up as I got close, like he didn't want me to notice him and he didn't want me to see that he was hurt. His appearance frightened me, so I left."

A week later the witness saw photos of Steven Diver on TV, then contacted the Erie County Sheriff's Office.

"With the exception of a somewhat heavier look under his chin and his hair slicked back and no glasses when I saw him on the bike path, I'm pretty sure it was the same person," she professed. "I'm ninety to ninety-five percent sure."

✳

Preschool class ended at 11:30 a.m., and ten minutes
before, parents began arriving to talk with the teacher
about the day's activities. Wendy Kelkenberg of Village
Daycare spoke to moms and dads and the kids waved
goodbye for the weekend, but Joan Diver was not there.
It was unusual for her to be late.

Kelkenberg knew the parents of all her students. The
prior Thursday, eight days earlier, Joan Diver had been
room mother for the morning, helping to organize activities and keep the play area clean.

On this day, Jennifer Christie served as room
mother. After other children filtered out, her daughter and Carter Diver were the only two remaining.
The two kids continued to play together. Within a
few minutes, Carter walked to the window with a
sense of foreboding and peered out for his mother.
Joan had still not arrived by 11:45. Kelkenberg called the
Diver house, but there was no response. She held up her
cell phone and asked Carter if his mom carried a phone
like it in her pocket. The boy shook his head. Kelkenberg
wondered if Carter's grandparents were nearby, but he
said they were in Idaho. Using the number on an emergency contact card, she called the university, but was
unable to reach Steven Diver directly. An operator transferred her to campus police, and Kelkenberg explained
the situation.

By 12:30 p.m., Joan was more than an hour late.
Christie, the room mother, had volunteered to stay with
her daughter so Carter had a playmate. But she needed

to leave. She offered to stop by Diver's house on the way home. Perhaps there was a simple explanation, a reason Joan was unable to answer the phone. When she pulled into Diver's driveway, there was no sign of activity. She peered through the front windows and saw an empty house. Although blinds covered the garage window, through a crease in the slats she saw the bare concrete floor. Christie asked a roofer next door if he had seen anyone coming or going. He had not, but admitted he hadn't been paying attention to the neighbor's house. Christie returned to her truck and called Kelkenberg to report her findings.

Kelkenberg's concern grew. Steven Diver phoned the day care shortly after Christie hung up. Campus security had just informed him of Joan's tardiness. He sensed something was wrong, and promised to pick up his son within twenty minutes. Before he left UB, he called the Erie County Sheriff's Office and asked them to check his house. He raced to his car and drove along Maple Road, frustrated by the slow pace of traffic. He arrived at the day care by 1:15.

When Diver took his son home, Joan was still not there. With his son secured in the car seat, he drove toward Main Street, looking for his wife's SUV along the way. Her Ford Explorer was parked in the lot on Salt Road, where she often began her workout, so he got out to check.

Pressing his face to the driver's side window, he tried the door handle, but it was locked and he had no key. The full water bottle inside suggested she had not yet returned from the run. A few steps away, just past a gradual curve, the path affords a clear view east for almost a half mile up the path. There was no sign of his wife.

At the far corner of the parking lot, in the only space darkened by shade, a white pickup angled beneath over-hanging limbs. The windows were rolled down, and a man reclined in the driver's seat. Diver did not approach him.

Diver worried that Joan had been injured during her run, and lay nearby, just off the trail, waiting for help. But the path snaked for eight miles through Clarence and Newstead, too far to cover effectively by foot. Back in the car, he raced north up Salt Road for home, called 911 and was told that a cruiser would be sent. As he hung up the phone, Kelkenberg pulled into the driveway, offering help. Diver handed her a phone and asked if she could stay with Carter. He changed from his button-down shirt into an old sweater and hastily loaded a bicycle into his trunk.

The 911 dispatcher had urged him to wait until a patrol car arrived, but Diver was in no mood for delay. He returned to the parking lot. A Honda Accord sporting a kayak rack had joined the white pickup, where a man still dozed with the window open. In his haste, Diver did not notice if the Ford Explorer remained in the lot. His only goal was to get on the path.

Town Highway Department workers received radio instructions to open the swinging metal gate at Salt Road. This would allow police cars access to the path. Two workers circled the parking lot in a truck, noticing aluminum wheels on a white pickup in the corner, and the roof rack on another car. Opening the gate, they saw a blond man unload a bicycle and begin pedaling east. He shouted "Joan" and then turned his head, listening for a response. Diver did not notice his wife's broken sunglasses concealed in the grass east of Davison Road.

Three miles from his starting point, a police car caught up to Diver where the bike path splits. Authorities had driven the trail, and found nothing out of the ordinary. In fact, they explained, Joan's Ford Explorer was not even in the Salt Road lot any longer.

Diver exhaled. Joan must have retrieved her SUV and returned home, although he had no idea where she might have been for the past two hours. The officers agreed to meet back at Diver's house to confirm everything was okay. They pulled away, and Diver pedaled his bike west. The path was deserted, and a light rain began to fall.

He returned home to find Kelkenberg playing with Carter, but there was no sign of Joan or her Explorer. No one could hazard a guess where the SUV was. When Diver's nine-year-old daughter was dropped off by the school bus, she listened to adults talk with concern about her missing mom.

The girl's first question was thick with anticipation. "Is she dead?"

Discovering the Body

Although Delano was not part of the initial investigation of Joan Diver's homicide, when the task force formed in the weeks following the murder, he and fellow detectives reviewed evidence and witness statements. Veteran officers who had encountered many grieving spouses

believed Steven Diver's behavior was unusual enough to
raise a red flag, beginning from the moment he learned
his wife disappeared.

"There were many strange aspects," Delano recalled.

One of the biggest had to do with Diver seeing his
wife's Explorer in the parking lot when he drove by the
first time. He had then rushed home to change clothes
and get his bike. Upon his return, he mounted the bike
and pedaled away. Later that day, Diver couldn't say for
sure if the Explorer was still there, but he did remember
seeing the white truck parked in the corner.

"Wouldn't you notice if your wife's vehicle was
gone?" Delano wondered. "The whole purpose of returning there was to search for her. It sounded fishy."

Diver's first pass through the Salt Road lot occurred
at approximately 1:30 p.m. A half hour later, when sheriff's deputies inspected the area, the SUV was no longer there. At 2:29 p.m., the vehicle was discovered three
miles away parallel to Shisler Road, south of Main Street,
adjacent to the bike path crossing.

At the trail intersection, there is no parking lot, just
a grassy pulloff large enough for a car. Across the street is
a lumber yard and an Ace Hardware store.

Although the vehicle was found, there was still no
sign of Joan.

"We later learned that the killer took keys from Joan
Diver's body and moved the SUV," Delano said. "When
Steven Diver peered inside his wife's truck, the guy was
probably right there in the woods watching. The killer
waited for the perfect opportunity to load his bike and
get out. He was careful, because no one saw him do it."

Moving the truck was intended to delay discovery of the body. The killer believed the search would begin around the spot the vehicle was found. This would buy time, because the actual crime scene was several miles east along the path.

The plan worked. It would be nearly forty-eight hours before Joan Diver was located.

One of the first officers to arrive at the scene on September 29 was Sergeant Greg Savage of the Erie County Sheriff's Office. In his mid-forties, Savage has a narrow face, with light brown hair cropped close to the scalp. His bright eyes and smooth face convey a youthful appearance. He began a law enforcement career in 1985 working as a guard at the Erie County Holding Center in downtown Buffalo—a history that would prove pivotal once he joined the task force and added his expertise to investigating old rape cases.

Savage runs the sheriff's SWAT team. Part of that duty includes search and rescue, so he was on location in Clarence when the call came about a missing woman.

"We began that night and worked until daylight," Savage recalled. "The center point of our search was where her SUV was found. We didn't know at the time that it had been moved by the killer."

Law enforcement officers examined the trail, searching with hand-held infrared devices, dogs, ATVs, and even a helicopter. There was no visible evidence of an abduction or attack. Between the darkness and the thick vines, finding a missing person became an improbable task.

"There is so much territory to cover," Savage noted. "It was nearly impossible to penetrate the brush. The night-time didn't help. We had volunteer firemen and teams of people going along slowly. Any area along the path with an opening in the foliage was examined thoroughly."

Steven Diver rode with the deputies and suggested locations to probe more closely. His cool, standoffish demeanor that night left officers wondering if he had played a role in his wife's disappearance.

"A couple of our investigators had Steven Diver in the car," Savage recalled. "We were going up and down the bike path and he was pointing out spots, saying this would be a good place to search for her. We wondered why he would say that unless he knew something. The guys who interviewed him suspected he was involved because he acted so weird."

At 8:30 p.m., in the back of a sheriff's car, Diver wrote a voluntary statement in which he reconstructed his day. He concluded, "Whatever happened to the truck, I think she was on the bike path running and something happened to her. If the truck was moved with the keys, then someone got the keys from her."

Steven Diver spent a sleepless night Friday. On Saturday morning, his wife's photo and an article about her disappearance was printed in the local section of the *Buffalo News*. A description of Joan Diver listed her at 5'5",

140 pounds, with green eyes and shoulder-length dark blonde hair.

The search continued Saturday with law enforcement officers and volunteers expanding their hunt along the trail, radiating farther from the SUV's discovery point on Shisler Road. By sunset, Joan Diver had yet to be located, although it was later learned that one searcher had come very close to her body, only to be shielded by thick undergrowth.

In spite of the resources employed during a two-day search, nothing of note had been uncovered. The sheriff's department had no evidence that a crime even occurred. Perhaps, for reasons only Joan Diver could explain, she had run away. Continuing the search seemed futile, and manpower was needed the following day for security at a Buffalo Bills football game. In a controversial decision, after examining the entire path for much of Friday and all of Saturday, the search was called off. The temporary command post at Clarence Fire Hall was closed.

"We felt at the time that we had exhausted all leads in the area," undersheriff Richard T. Donovan explained to the media later.

That night, family and friends gathered at the Diver house to formulate a plan. The group agreed to organize another search party and post announcements in local churches on Sunday morning. By noon, approximately one hundred volunteers assembled at the Salt Road parking lot, where Joan's SUV had been parked two days earlier. Maps were handed out, and volunteers broke into a dozen groups that examined different areas of the trail.

In mid-afternoon, walking down the clearing at the pipeline between Davison and Barnum Roads, a volunteer ducked into a heavily wooded area and spotted white sneakers. Through a tangle of leaves and grasses, a body lay on its back. Glimpsing blonde hair, he called to a fellow searcher.

"Sir, I found something here," he said. "There's a body here."

Another searcher, a scout master to the Divers' children who had been present at their house the night before, stepped forward.

"Her legs were bare but she still had on a shirt and a blue sweatshirt that was draped over her," the second man recalled. "I looked long enough to verify that it was Joan Diver, then backed away into the pipeline area and called on a walkie-talkie."

The two kept a vigil until sheriff's deputies arrived to secure the scene.

Savage had been working the Bills game that day, and around 4:30 p. m. was informed that a body was found in Clarence.

"It hadn't been identified yet, but who else could it be?" Savage asked.

He went to the bike path and assembled a team to conduct grid searches around the crime scene. Recruits from the police academy lined up elbow to elbow and covered the whole area on hands and knees looking for any kind of clue. Joan Diver's broken sunglasses were recovered, but nothing else. The police secured the crime scene and used alternate light sources to search for stray semen, but nothing was found.

Ironically, Savage had been part of a team who searched that very area the day before. He was posted on the south side of the path, but Diver's body lay in a gully to the north.

"There was some question later if the body had been put there after we did the search," Savage said. "Nobody knew what went on. I don't think that's the case. I believe that's where she was killed. She wasn't that far off the bike path but it was a heavily wooded area. She should have been discovered earlier."

Finding the body put to rest any theories that Joan Diver might have fled her home. But now the question loomed: Who murdered her?

Three days before Joan Diver's murder, a mysterious envelope arrived at Buffalo police headquarters. It had no return address but contained a photocopy of a 2005 article from the *Buffalo News* about the Bike Path Rapist.

"This was a pretty lengthy story from the newspaper," Delano explained. "It talked about how after analyzing DNA from the 1994 rape, there was no sperm discovered. There had been sperm in the previous attack in 1992, so that indicated within a two-year period he either had a vasectomy or testicular cancer. At that time, we didn't know what happened, but the newspaper highlighted that this was an important revelation."

The envelope was addressed to headquarters, where it was unsealed. On the back of the article was printed the name "Arnold Ware"* with a Crescent Avenue address.

No one was sure what this meant, so it was forwarded to the Sex Offense Squad, where the Bike Path Rapist case had gone cold because there had been no attacks since 1994.

"What's strange is that someone had saved that article from a year earlier," Delano said. "The printing looked like it came from a handicapped person. Big letters, like the way a child writes. We didn't know what to make of it, so we went looking for Arnold Ware."

Ware no longer lived on Crescent Avenue. He was found in a West Seneca apartment, a recluse whose only income came from public assistance. He did not drive, wore long hair and a longer beard, and there was no TV or computer in his home.

"He was slow on the uptake, kind of spaced out," Delano said. "Like a throwback to the 1960s. He was smoking pot because we found roaches in the ashtray. We talked to him twice, but he claimed to have no knowledge of how that letter got to us."

Investigators were puzzled. The serial rapist had not been heard from for twelve years, but Ware was not a viable suspect. Who had sent this mysterious note? What was its purpose?

"If you put it into context, it's very unusual," Delano noted. "All these years go by between attacks, and suddenly a clue shows up three days before a killing. We sent it to the lab to be processed, but nobody could explain that letter."

Did Arnold Ware have any connection to the Bike Path Rapist?

Suspects

Some observers recognized the significance of the date. On September 29, 1990, University at Buffalo student Linda Yalem, age twenty-two, had been raped and strangled, the first known killing attributed to the Bike Path Rapist. Although the attacker was still at large, there had been no forensic evidence linking him to a crime since 1994. Was it possible that he chose the sixteen-year anniversary to resume murder?

Many were skeptical. The connections seemed murky. Three significant factors—the date, use of a ligature, and an assault along a rural bike trail—all matched the prior m.o. But the murder happened in a town where the Bike Path Rapist had never struck before. No rape had occurred, and sexual assault had always been the killer's prime motivation. Lacking that, any link seemed to be a stretch.

The *Buffalo News* believed the date to be an "eerie coincidence." Those in law enforcement were aware of the association, but it was a point of discussion rather than a solid connection.

As yet, there had been no DNA found at the scene to prove the Bike Path Rapist's involvement. Besides, that case had been cold for a dozen years.

✳

After his wife's SUV was remanded to custody, Steven Diver would not consent to a police search of the vehicle. By Thursday, October 5, the *Buffalo News* reported that Diver was "less cooperative," but not a person of interest. The same day, a warrant was secured to inspect the truck.

The SUV had been stored at a secure facility during the idle six days. Now the truck underwent processing that invoked forensic scenes from a prime-time TV drama. Crime scene investigators examined every inch of the vehicle, both inside and out. All scratches, nicks, and dents on the exterior were photographed and cataloged as potential evidence. Masking tape was stretched across upholstery to pick up stray hairs, fibers, and loose particles. Swabs were taken from all the spots that came in frequent contact with skin—the steering wheel, door handles, and key slot.

A team of three Erie County sheriffs worked for an entire eight-hour shift over Columbus Day weekend. Deputy James Mirusso joined detectives Kevin Mahoney and Steve Meerboth for the detailed task. Mirusso's expertise was required. Previously a crime scene investigator, his job had been eliminated during a county budget crunch. He had been bumped to road patrol but was invited back to assist and utilize his processing skills.

By day's end, accumulated evidence was turned over to the Central Police Services (CPS) forensic lab for analysis.

The prevailing theory was that whoever killed Joan Diver had moved her SUV. Although there was no semen or blood unearthed at the crime scene, perhaps the vehicle would contain some particle of evidence to pinpoint a suspect.

Until lab results became available, investigators spent their days pursuing leads, committed to snaring Joan Diver's killer.

Beginning in the spring of 2006, regular hikers of the Clarence Bike Path noticed a suspicious person along the trail. Several citizens were concerned enough that they called authorities to report strange behavior in the weeks before Joan Diver's murder.

The subject was described as approximately thirty years old, between 5'8" and 5'10", with a bronze complexion from an artificial tan. He had the lean frame of a distance runner, wearing a dark cap, oversized sunglasses, and a music player strapped against his arm, cords snaking to his ears. He was noticeable because of his awkward jogging technique. When he ran, his legs splayed out to the sides, rather than pumping forward and backward.

But his wardrobe choices caused observers to do a double take. There was a turban wrapped around his nose and mouth concealing the lower half of his face. He also wore a black bikini bottom that wedged as he ran, exposing his hips and buttocks.

"I don't know if suspicious is a good word, just weird, offbeat, looking for attention the way he was dressed," one woman wrote in a statement to police.

From a distance it was thought the jogger was female due to the thin body and bikini bottom. The covered jaw only added to the androgyny. But upon closer examination, all who encountered him noticed muscular arms and hairy legs.

According to witnesses, he avoided eye contact, averting his face and stepping off the trail when someone approached. He darted in and out of the woods. Some theorized he went into the brush to urinate, but several times he was seen entering the treeline wearing a bikini bottom and emerging quickly covered by longer shorts.

Concerned for the safety of his wife, who frequented the path, a Clarence resident followed him one day in August 2006, watching the runner move west toward Salt Road, cross Main Street near Sawmill Road, and get into a black Toyota parked behind a gas station. The license number was recorded and given to the Erie County Sheriff's Department.

"He may be just an innocent serious runner, but it seems odd that he never parks in the lot near the path," a witness e-mailed the sheriff's office. "He must feel it is inappropriate to wear the thong while getting in and out of his car, but it is okay to wear it on the path."

In their vernacular, cops began referring to the runner as "the thong guy."

On the morning of September 29, 2006, three separate people spotted this jogger on the trail near the spot Joan Diver's body was later discovered.

"Initially we thought the thong guy was a prime suspect for the murder," Greg Savage reflected. "He's a wacky guy to begin with, running around with his ass hanging out, and he's on the bike path just about every day. We're thinking he's running because he likes to chase girls around. And we have witnesses that morning who put him at the spot she's killed."

The suspect, Ross Hanson,* was an unemployed thirty-year-old living in a motel on Main Street in Clarence. Estranged from his family, who had moved to Virginia, Hanson earned a bachelor's degree from Canisius College in Buffalo and had been a medical student at UB for two years before leaving school. He admitted suffering from dyslexia and attention deficit/hyperactivity disorder. He had no girlfriend, and claimed to support himself by mowing lawns and shoveling snow.

When Hanson drove to the Sheriff's Detective Bureau in downtown Buffalo on Tuesday, October 10, for a voluntary interview, officers were certain they had Joan Diver's killer within their grasp.

The meeting began conversationally, with a deputy and detective asking a series of background questions. At various times during the next several hours, Savage and Lieutenant Ron Kenyon also participated.

Sheriffs tried to establish a rapport, but Hanson remained distant and noncommittal. He became upset recounting alienation from his family, especially his recent exclusion from his sister's wedding. He told investigators that he averaged forty miles of running per week, and the exercise provided relief from his life's problems.

He provided no explanation for wearing a thong during his workout. The gag, however, was called a "cool wrap," purchased at a local sporting goods store. He said that when moistened and wrapped around the face, it helped prevent dehydration.

Officers were concerned that Hanson did not ask why he was being questioned. When pressed if he might have information about the recent homicide, he said little, claiming to be ignorant of the murder. All he had heard was that a woman was found dead by the side of a road.

The interviewers weren't buying his explanation, especially when they noticed pulsing arteries on his neck. The Diver murder had been a major news event for the past eleven days. They believed it unlikely Hanson was ignorant of it, considering that he regularly used the very path on which she was killed.

He ran the trail during the morning of September 29, he admitted, but near Clarence Town Park, several miles west of where the body was discovered. He insisted he was nowhere near Davison and Barnum Roads, an area he called "the extension." He even sketched a map showing his route that day.

"He was lying to us and we knew it," Savage recalled.

Where the pipeline crossed the bike path, at the spot Joan Diver's body was found, a clearing opens into the back of a poultry farm. A witness at the barn there saw a runner in a thong cross Davison Road heading east. Hanson said he parked his car on Main Street and was going the other way, toward Clarence Town Park.

"He completely put himself away from the murder scene, which indicated to us that he was guilty," Savage said. "If he didn't do it, why didn't he just say he was there but didn't see a thing?"

Throughout the interview, Hanson was cautious, especially about leaving DNA samples. Over the course of several hours, he was given a bottle of water, a cup of coffee, and a bottle of root beer. He kept the three containers with him, even when moving between rooms, and became frustrated with the logistics of simultaneously grasping all three at once. He made sure his sleeves were down and his skin was covered before resting his arms on any flat surfaces.

Hanson moved into Savage's office to record a statement, setting the coffee cup on the floor. While the suspect's attention was diverted, Savage quietly nabbed it and hid it from sight. When that interview was finished and they prepared to move to another room, Hanson scanned the floor for the cup. He did not want to draw attention or ask where it had gone, so he reluctantly left without it. Savage in turn tagged the cup as evidence and submitted it to Central Police Services to run a DNA profile.

While Hanson was being interviewed at the sheriff's office on West Eagle Street in downtown Buffalo, fellow officers searched the surrounding roads and parking garages for his car. They planned to run a scent test using Billie T, a bloodhound from the Niagara County Sheriff's Department. This might provide clues as to Hanson's involvement in the Diver homicide and also bolster the application for a search warrant of Hanson's property, if necessary.

Hanson's Toyota was discovered parked on West Genesee near Fourth Street. Using a gauze pad taken from the front seat of Joan Diver's SUV, the dog matched a scent and began following an invisible route, crossing a lawn to Church Street, wandering through the parking lot of the Channel 7 TV studios and back onto the road. After continuing through a stoplight onto West Eagle Street, the bloodhound traced a byway directly to the door of the detective bureau.

According to the subsequent application for a search warrant, "The actions of the dog suggested that the last person to drive [Joan Diver's] Ford Explorer on September 29, 2006, was also recently in the vicinity of Hanson's vehicle and had entered the front door of 134 West Eagle Street."

Back in the interview room, Hanson maintained that he was nowhere near Davison Road on the morning of Diver's murder. In fact, he claimed to remember a temperature drop while he was close to the path's intersection at Shisler Road, three miles west of the crime scene. He mentioned the lumber yard and hardware store nearby. This was where Joan Diver's SUV had been discovered after its mysterious move.

Hanson's comments and the findings of the bloodhound opened a new line of questioning. Could Hanson have driven the SUV away from the Salt Road parking lot? After advising him of his Miranda rights, the sheriffs' tone quickly changed as they confronted him about inconsistencies. Questions came fast and furious now, and Hanson seemed overwhelmed.

Q: What do you think should be the punishment for the person who murdered Joan Diver?

A: I don't know . . .

Q: Did you ever enter Joan Diver's vehicle?

A: No.

Q: Would you enter someone's car if it wasn't yours?

A: No.

Q: Are you trying to protect someone else?

A: No.

Q: Have you ever seen Joan Diver?

A: I don't think so. Do you have a picture of her?

A photo of Diver with her daughter was provided. Then several crime scene snapshots were spread across the table. Diver's stripped body lay in the underbrush, blonde head turned to the side while a jacket covered her midsection. Hanson's hands trembled and he began to cry.

We know you killed Joan Diver, the interviewers said, *but we don't know whether it was premeditated or accidental. The family, especially the four children, need closure. Only you can provide it.*

A rash rose along Hanson's neck. He slouched forward, kept his head down, and clutched his stomach while rocking back and forth.

Q: May we search your car?

A: No.

Q: May we search your apartment?

A: No.

Q: Will you provide a DNA sample?

A: No.

Q: Take a polygraph?

A: No.

Q: Why not?

Silence.

If you're innocent, all these things could clear you, investigators explained.

Still, there was no response.

Hanson finally asked what Joan Diver did for a living, how many children she had, and where her husband worked.[4] When told of the bloodhound's discovery and the theory that he had driven the victim's SUV, he had no explanation.

Suddenly, Hanson had a change of heart. Perhaps being expelled from his family was less frightening than the accusations leveled at him. Hanson asked to speak to his dad. The detective phoned him, and father and son spoke privately. The sheriffs' questions stopped when Hanson announced he would retain an attorney.

"One of his relatives who lives locally called and asked how far we were going to push this," sheriff's

---

[4] Investigators searched for a connection through the University at Buffalo. Hanson had once been enrolled there; Steven Diver was a professor in the chemistry department. There was no apparent link, however. It is unlikely the two knew of each other.

detective Alan Rozansky recalled. "At that point, I wasn't sure what he did or didn't do, but I explained this was a homicide and he was a legitimate suspect."

A week later, a search warrant was issued for Hanson's apartment. When sheriff's deputies arrived, Hanson was reluctant to allow them entry, but relented after phoning his lawyer. A sour stench permeated the room, and it appeared Hanson was in the middle of moving. Sheets had been removed from the bed, drawers were emptied, and flattened cardboard boxes leaned against a wall. Although a computer and VHS tapes were confiscated, none provided a link to the killing.

Using security video from the motel, sheriffs were able to determine the times Hanson departed and returned to his room on the morning of September 29.

"'Thong Boy' was a phenomenal suspect," admitted Erie County assistant district attorney Ken Case, who prepared search warrants for Hanson's room. "He jogged on the path every day. When his room was searched, we found videos of naked women wrestling. There was a water bottle with what appeared to be a spot of blood. Investigators had narrowed the window when Joan Diver was killed to two hours. He claimed to be in his room during those two hours, but we checked the surveillance cameras and he was out. I thought, *case closed*."

Detectives also learned that the day after Joan Diver's death, a Dumpster fire occurred at the motel. Had Hanson destroyed evidence that would connect him to murder?

While some believed he was involved, many people became more skeptical as weeks passed.

"For a couple days early on, we thought he was the killer," Rozansky said. "But he was a strange bird. He admitted his silence had to do with not upsetting his family. He had enough mental problems that if we asked when Martians landed, he might have said yesterday. We never stopped looking at him, but the longer we talked to him, it became clear that he was in another world."

Joan Diver's blue fleece covered her body from chest to pubic area. A footprint was discovered on the fabric, an indentation as if someone had stepped on the body. Her running shorts were gathered around one ankle, with that leg bent at the knee.

Even after the killer's capture, there are details that have yet to be explained. Why was Joan Diver not raped? Who covered her with her own jacket?

"There are all these little crazy pieces of the puzzle that don't line up," Savage explained.

"I don't believe the Bike Path Rapist covered her body, even though he later admitted it," Delano noted. "That illustrates remorse and compassion. This guy had no remorse or compassion. He says he did it so that she was less likely to be discovered, but I'm not buying it. Using a blue jacket to cover someone in the woods would only draw more attention. She'd be less noticeable if she was left uncovered."

One theory that detectives considered was that Hanson saw or heard part of the struggle between Diver and her attacker. Witnesses spotted him near the scene, running in place close to the attack site. Perhaps Diver was not raped because the killer suddenly realized another person was watching nearby. Both Hanson and the murderer later denied that ever happened.

"We think Hanson either saw the killer on the path, or interrupted the crime, which is why she wasn't raped," Savage said. "He may have seen her body and threw the sweatshirt over her. After we arrested the Bike Path Rapist, we wanted to talk to the thong guy again. His lawyer said he would talk if we granted him immunity. Why does he need immunity? What did he do? We don't know what his role was. Since then he's refused to talk to us. Did he stumble upon the attack? Did he find her? I don't know how he would because she was off in the bushes, but something just doesn't add up."

Hanson was not the only suspect. Questions lingered about Steven Diver, and the UB professor did little to allay police concerns.

Standard procedure in a homicide is to investigate family members first, if only to rule them out as suspects. With the discovery of his wife's body, Steven Diver's life became the subject of police scrutiny. His aloof demeanor, in addition to conflicting reports about him gathered in the days to come, caused detectives to consider his role in the killing.

"Steven Diver made himself a perfect suspect," Delano revealed. "On the morning of the homicide, he was supposedly in a lab, but nobody saw him because he locked himself in to do experiments. We didn't know if he was there or out killing his wife. Then, when he learned Joan didn't pick their son up from day care, instead of calling 911, he called the sheriff's substation in Clarence. Wouldn't you call 911 if you thought your wife was in danger?"

Before his wife was discovered, Diver sketched a detailed map of the bike path. His knowledge of the area represented more than a passing interest. He had spent time on that trail and knew it thoroughly. Was that information gleaned from scouting locations ahead of time?

"He knew that path like the back of his hand," Delano said. "He was drawing things like benches and bridges. The detail was precise."

Diver circled two locations on the map, suggesting sheriffs concentrate their search within those regions. Joan was found within one of the circles. Was it a coincidence or did her husband have inside information?

"Steven Diver was questioned but that's part of the procedure," Rozansky explained. "You start by questioning the spouse. It doesn't mean you don't look at other people too, but Steven Diver was offended by it."

Armed with information from a fellow professor, who saw Diver emerge from a lab that morning behaving strangely, sheriffs searched the building's garbage, thinking perhaps evidence had been discarded there. They found nothing.

"Diver is a different type of guy," Rozansky said. "He would not let bloodhounds around his house. He refused to allow us entry to his vehicle. He forced us to get a search warrant to examine his wife's SUV. Why would you do that? He refused a lie detector test. He was advised by fellow professors to hire an attorney, so he secured one right away."

Public speculation grew as Diver sequestered himself. The University at Buffalo released him from teaching duties for the semester, and Diver became increasingly wary of authorities.

"We felt that the detectives were not listening to our initial concerns that Joan may have been attacked on the bike path," said Professor Huw Davies, a colleague and friend of Steven Diver. "They were focusing simply on domestic issues and infidelities. At the time we had no confidence in the police and I suggested to Steve that he retain an attorney."

"It was crazy because everybody thought the husband had something to do with it," Savage recalled. "With a missing woman, that's usually the case."

But a single spot of DNA discovered in Joan's SUV shifted the focus in an entirely different direction.

Politics of a Task Force

Timothy Howard, the Erie County sheriff, received a shocking report from Central Police Services on November 15, 2006. A swab taken from the steering wheel of Joan Diver's SUV recovered a single droplet of sweat. After comparing DNA markers, it was confirmed that the perspiration belonged to the Bike Path Rapist.

This news pointed to what investigators suspected: Joan Diver's killer likely moved her vehicle after the murder, not knowing he left behind a conclusive piece of evidence. Now there was proof linking this crime to the phantom who had terrorized a community two decades earlier.

After a dozen years of silence, he was back.

He spent hours of free time at the Butler-Mitchell Boys Club on Buffalo's west side, playing basketball and ping-pong or shooting pool. The competition kept him occupied after school. During his formative years, the Boys Club was his life. Being there kept him rooted and because of that, he felt connected to the community.

"I was a happy kid, but I was shy. I had trouble concentrating in school. Very low grades. I had blackouts where I couldn't remember what had happened two hours ago. This started happening in high school. Around my junior or senior year, I felt a lot of anger inside and I couldn't control it. After my senior year is when I started my rapes. I took out my anger on other people that I never knew."

Throughout high school, he never had a girlfriend.

"I would go to school, do my sports, and come back home. I never had too many friends, guys or girls. I was more of a lonely person. When I started these crimes, I don't know what made me do it. I was happy with what I was doing before. I don't know what made me turn into what I am now."

As high school came to a close, acquaintances at the Boys Club urged him to continue in education. After lettering in baseball at Grover Cleveland High School, he pitched for two years at Buffalo State College until the baseball program was cancelled. During his second year, he met Kathleen, the woman who would become his wife.

"To be honest, my first girlfriend was my wife. I was afraid to approach a woman and talk to her. But when I was in college, I lived in one of the towers near the Scajaqueda.[5] Girls were on one side, boys on the other. I met my wife when she was a freshman. I used to play catch with these girls, and one of them came up and said a friend of hers wanted to talk to me."

They soon began dating and he was smitten. Kathleen's mother passed away during her first year at college, and he supported her through the emotional time. She

---

[5] This is a nickname for a highway that runs through Buffalo.

lived nearby in an apartment with her brother. With the discovery she was pregnant, he left school, taking a job so they could support the baby.

"I knew I was falling in love and she would make me happy. I was married twenty-seven years. There was not one time when this anger crossed my mind with her. She never knew my dark side. I never laid a hand on my wife. The rapes I committed always had to do with someone I never knew. If you were my friend or next-door neighbor, you never saw anger hit me. It came to me when I was alone. That's when I started committing these rapes."

When he reached his mid-twenties, the anger escalated to the point where it scared him. He could not explain the cause and felt his behavior was out of control. Yet he did not know how to stop. He never told anyone or sought help.

"Around 1984 or 1985, each time I did something it got worse and worse. I never wanted to hurt nobody. I just wanted to get my urge out."

Releasing pent-up rage came in the form of ejaculation. He claims that in his early attacks, he did not penetrate his victim, but simply held her down and rubbed himself against her. That soon escalated to rape.

"I know some of these girls I raped, they never hurt nobody." He paused, shaking his head in disbelief. "What I did, I blame myself for a lot of it, for all that happened. They didn't hurt nobody."

He stared silently, face draped with a vacant expression, as if his confession was an epiphany.

✳

With a square face and gray hair, sheriff's detective Alan Rozansky is a wiry, compact man whose movements are staccato punctuations. His gait is quick, his eyes darting, and he speaks fast, often jumping between subjects and leaving sentences to dangle unfinished. Rozansky began police work as a nineteen-year-old during a period of campus unrest in the 1970s. While a student, he worked undercover gathering intelligence about subversive activities at the University at Buffalo. After graduating from UB and then the police academy, he spent much of his career investigating narcotics, embracing the character by growing a beard and long hair.

"It took CPS six weeks to process that DNA analysis," recalled Rozansky, who, in his mid-fifties, is now clean-shaven with thinning hair. "They treated it like it was routine. When they learned they were dealing with the Bike Path Rapist, it wasn't routine anymore. After that, everything we gave them came back quickly, within forty-eight hours."

Revelation of the serial killer's involvement forced the investigation to shift. Before DNA results, there were two primary suspects: Hanson and Diver. Once it was proven the Bike Path Rapist was involved, the case went in a different direction. Neither was likely to be the long-sought killer.

"Steven Diver isn't from this area, so the odds of him doing rapes and murders here in the '80s and '90s was long," Rozansky said. "And Hanson was only thirty, which ruled him out because of his age. He wouldn't have been old enough twenty and twenty-five years ago. At that point we had to think less of them."

News of the Bike Path Rapist's return sent ripples of shock throughout Western New York. But some in law enforcement were not surprised, given the nature of the attack.

"The day that Joan Diver went missing, I believed he was back," reflected Lissa Redmond, a detective who spent several years in Buffalo's Sex Crimes Unit trying to solve the Bike Path Rapist's last known attack in 1994. "I knew it was him when we went to the sheriff and saw Polaroids they had taken at the murder site."

In addition to strangulation marks, the date, and a connection to a bike path, the placement of Diver's body was consistent with past cases.

"You're always worried about a copycat, but this couldn't have been because details about the body had never been made public," Redmond said. "There were many people who were convinced the husband did it. I wasn't one of them."

Although he appeared unlikely to have killed his wife, investigators were not ready to rule out Diver yet. Delano explained that a number of improbable scenarios were examined. One of the most bizarre was based on opportunity: In the course of his job as a science professor, Diver had worked with DNA.

"We kicked around the question whether Steven Diver could have gotten the Bike Path Rapist's DNA and put it in his own vehicle. What if he killed his wife and planted the DNA to throw us off track? It sounds absurd, but during an investigation, you have to look at all the angles you can think of. He had the ability to manipulate or hide DNA."

Detectives contacted the CPS lab, where the DNA was stored. They were told it was not possible for Diver to have access to the Bike Path Rapist's sample.

"That technology began to be used in the 1980s," Delano explained. "What if twenty years ago that DNA was sent to UB for tests or experiments and Diver somehow got his hands on it? We were assured that was impossible. We also wondered if the Divers were acquaintances of the Bike Path Rapist, not knowing he was a serial killer. We tried to find out who else had driven that SUV before Joan's murder."

Rozansky contends that even before DNA results came back, investigators considered Diver less of a suspect than they had initially. Several witnesses claimed he was on campus between noon and 12:30. The time frame for him to have committed the crime was too narrow to be realistic.

"As much as he was being uncooperative, he just did not have a window of time," Rozansky said. "For him to go up to Newstead, attack his wife and come back, a whole lot of people would have had to lie about seeing him at UB."

Discovery of the Bike Path Rapist's DNA laid to rest one of the prevailing theories of the past dozen years: He was still alive. But it opened avenues for many more questions. What had he been doing? Where was he? And most importantly, how could he be caught?

"Positive DNA for the Bike Path Rapist came back on Wednesday, November 15," recalled chief Scott Patronik of the Erie County Sheriff's Department. "Timothy Howard got a call early in the day, and this flipped an ignition switch. Until then, there had been some question if it was really him. Before 8:00 a.m., the sheriff called police chiefs in Amherst, Buffalo, and anywhere that a rape had occurred."

Howard informed his fellow supervisors that there was a DNA link and recommended combining a team of investigators from different jurisdictions. Collaboration and shared resources were needed to capture the killer. The five-year statute of limitations had expired on his last known rape in 1994, so he could not be prosecuted for any sexual assaults. But there were three murders for which he could always be charged.

"We knew the guy was here and active, so this was the time to get him," Patronik recalled.

A press conference announcing formation of a task force was held the following day. The Amherst police were quick to take the lead. John Moslow, Amherst's chief of police, suggested the team be headquartered in his building.

Four detectives composed the initial investigative unit: Delano, Rozansky, Amherst detective Ed Monan, and state police investigator Josh Keats. The men gathered in a cramped room, and within days, tension threatened to shatter their unity.

Assemble a group of adults and ask them to solve a problem, and odds are there will be disagreements over the best approach. Even when all parties desire success, there may be personality conflicts, quarrels, and harsh words. Uneasy feelings may linger after the job is complete.

So it is with cops. The early days of the task force, working from the Amherst police station, were a time of friction. The investigation diverged as everyone followed a different track. Consensus proved elusive.

"You get a bunch of cops together and we're like little kids," Delano admitted. "There are too many egos, so we clashed. A few of the people I worked with were a pain in the ass and I wasn't shy about telling them to their faces."

The Amherst police were anxious to be included among the task force, because several attacks had occurred within the township years before. The department had a chip on its shoulder because Linda Yalem's case had remained unsolved for sixteen years. In spite of her rape and murder, Amherst has been voted one of the nation's safest communities. Violent crime in the town is rare, so when it does occur, police take it to heart.

"We don't get many murders in Amherst," admitted Detective Lieutenant Joseph LaCorte.[6] Some task force members criticized the way Amherst handled the investigation, claiming their inexperience with homicides became obvious. It was later learned that the killer's name was buried within reams of Amherst's files, and he had come to the station in 1991 for a voluntary interview but had been allowed to go free after an hour of questioning.

---

[6] Besides the Bike Path Rapist case, another murder in Amherst received international attention. In 1998, Dr. Barnett Slepian, an abortion provider, was shot through a window in his home with a high-powered rifle. His killer, James Kopp, was eventually captured in France, extradited to the United States, and convicted of murder.

LaCorte is a tall, thin man in his mid-fifties whose job is to oversee the detective bureau. Rounded gold-rimmed glasses sit atop a prominent nose. His face is bony and angular, reminiscent of the man in the American Gothic painting. He embraces formality, courteously referring to people—even murderers—by the title of "Mr." or "Mrs." LaCorte dresses elegantly, regularly donning a suit and tie, and a gold ring decorates his pinky finger. Although quick to smile and laugh, there is a sober undertone to him. This is a serious man who treats police work with gravity.

LaCorte and other bosses in Amherst believed the best way to crack the case was by soliciting tips from citizens. Someone out there had to know something. *America's Most Wanted* televised an episode about the Bike Path Rapist, and more than two thousand leads poured in from across the nation. Amherst police were insistent that each tip be thoroughly researched; they were confident that clues to the criminal's capture lay dormant within the mass of information.

"We assembled something like four thousand names based on tips," LaCorte noted. Already his department had shelves of paperwork, filling some fifteen three-inch binders with information. "Many of the names were repeats, and others were crackpots looking to frame someone they were angry with. Still, all the names needed to be cleared."

LaCorte, Captain Timothy Green and Senior Clerk-Typist Sandy Roehrig were the three people who saw every tip. Roehrig typed each lead into a computer that categorized the data. Studying old case files and investigating tips would be the starting point.

Soon it became evident that there was not enough manpower to run down all the leads. Some leads were easy to clear; others required a return phone call to solicit more information. Clearing one lead could take up to four hours. The process was time consuming, but necessary, because investigators only needed to be successful once.

Josh Keats of the state police is trim and fit, his sandy-colored brush cut beginning to fleck gray on the sides. He is in his mid-thirties, making him one of the younger members of the task force. He joined the state police in 1994. His regular job is to work the violent crimes investigative team, which deals with homicides and violent felonies, assisting local police as needed.

"My belief was that the name of the killer was buried somewhere in the existing files," Keats recalled. "Somebody had to have it already, whether it was Amherst or the sheriff or Buffalo. State police would not have it because we had never investigated this case. I told Lieutenant LaCorte to get ready for that revelation because it was going to happen."

Keats believes that he was invited onto the task force because of his ability to cooperate with other officers, but that everyone on the team did not share that trait. Tension soon mounted between Keats and Delano.

"Dennis Delano is experienced, knowledgeable, and wants to do the right thing," Keats said. "But when he doesn't get his way, he goes off on his own. That's not the way to work a case like this."

✳

With conflicting personalities and different opinions on how to solve a long-standing open file, it is no wonder that tempers flared quickly. Delano, Rozansky, and Keats shared the narrow edges of a single desk. Delano spread files in a semicircle on the floor around him and laid a flat plank across his lap as a portable workstation.

"I was bitching from day one that our space was too small," Delano recalled. "They had a big empty classroom nearby so I said, 'What's wrong with this room?' I was told they used that area for other stuff. I said, 'I hope it's more important than trying to solve three homicides.'"

A sense of humor shines through when Delano recounts the conflicts.

"On the first day, I asked if there was coffee anywhere. You had to pay for coffee. It was only a quarter, but I immediately took a burn to that," he said with a chuckle, shaking his head. "It became one of my pet peeves. They invite us there and then ask us to pay? If you come to my house, I'll give you free coffee. You won't have to pay for it. I knew I was making waves, but I had nothing to lose."

Visiting officers were to run all new information by Amherst bosses, a plan that did not sit well with veteran cops from different jurisdictions. One of the biggest issues was the pecking order. Who assigned tips to be investigated? Did certain officers receive "hotter" tips than others? Was one agency pulling stronger leads in the hopes of claiming credit when the case was complete?

"Most of the task force had the opinion that if we solved any of these three homicides, we'd solve them all," Delano proclaimed. "Amherst was solely working on the

Yalem case. If they encountered another homicide that connected to Yalem that was okay, but it was like they had to be the agency that solved it instead of working as a team. I had a blowout and walked out of there."

Delano phoned his boss, chief of detectives Dennis Richards. He explained the situation was not working. Richards requested that Delano return to his desk in downtown Buffalo.

"I felt they were withholding information and cherry-picking the best leads," Delano noted with frustration in his voice. "When I'm working a homicide, I don't play these little games. It's a serious thing for me. I stormed away, refusing to spend any more time there."

Rozansky agreed with Delano's opinion.

"Neither Dennis nor I felt comfortable," he said. "I live nearby and have many friends in the Amherst police, but things didn't feel right. We were given tape recorders, told to record our work on them and hand it to the station's secretary, who would type it up. I'm not a defiant guy. I'm a team player, but I didn't like the situation. We weren't there to make our case and hand it to Amherst so they could solve Linda Yalem. The ultimate goal was to get the Bike Path Rapist, and I think some people lost sight of that."

Frustrated at what he believed were back-room politics by fellow law enforcers, Delano returned to Franklin Street, where he began pulling unsolved rape files. He assembled a chart that tracked dates, times, victims, and methods of attack. This ever-evolving blueprint provided a big-picture view, and would be a key component to catching the killer.

"All the policemen came to the task force with years
of experience," LaCorte explained. "Some of us wanted to
cover tips in a different way. We're all adults, so that was
fine with me, but my job was to prioritize and have people clear them. There were checks and balances. Sometimes I would think there was more to do to clear a tip, so
I requested that a person dig deeper."

Patronik, the Erie County Sheriff's Department chief
whose charge was to oversee the task force, realized that
the unit was crumbling. With progress stalled early, the
game plan needed major revisions, and fast.

Assembling on Oak Street

Near the corner of Walden Avenue and Harlem Road in Cheektowaga, he nudged his vehicle close to the sliding doors of Home Depot. Here a teenager wearing an orange apron helped him stack plywood onto the roof. They laid thick pieces of cloth against the car to ensure its paint was not scratched. The store employee secured the wood together, wrapping it tightly with a nylon cord.

As he drove a few blocks toward home, he savored the dark knowledge. The rope would be perfect.

A knife or a gun left too many opportunities for error. That girl on the railroad overpass had grabbed at the gun when he set it down, bashing his head with the handle and leaving a welt the size of a half-dollar. He had been careless, for sure. Thankfully, she had not squeezed the trigger and he was able to wrestle the weapon back from her.

He wouldn't make that mistake again.

A movie on TV gave him the idea. Approach from behind and slip a garrote over the victim's head. By alternately choking and releasing pressure, he could control the woman and bring her in and out of consciousness. If she struggled or made too much noise, just pull a bit tighter to compress her windpipe. She would become obedient real quickly.

Back home, he unloaded the wood and propped it against the garage wall. With his wife at work and kids at school, he snapped on a fluorescent light and began in earnest. He sawed a broom handle into two six-inch sections, long enough that they would fit snugly in his palms without wriggling from his grip. Then he twisted rope around the handles, securing it with black electrical tape, keeping it straight and hard. There was enough rope—two or three feet—to loop around someone's neck twice.

When he was finished, he had a weapon that was highly practical. It was easy to carry, collapsing so it was small enough to fit in a jacket pocket. It would also be simple to take it apart and dispose of the components once an attack was done.

The double ligature became his signature.

Between September 29 and November 15, Lieutenant Ron Kenyon of the Erie County Sheriff's Department supervised the Diver homicide. He was on the scene the weekend Joan went missing, and interviewed suspects during the following six weeks. But Kenyon had prior involvement with other homicide investigations and found his attention pulled in several directions.

When DNA results were announced, it became obvious this case would be far more complex than first expected. Someone needed to oversee this full time, so Scott Patronik was invited into the fold.

"The sheriff, Tim Howard, asked me over lunch if I could work on the Bike Path Rapist case full time," Patronik recalled. "I thought, great, this thing has been open for more than twenty years. It probably won't be a ringing success, but when I was assigned, Ron went back to working other cases."[7]

Scott Patronik is an unobtrusive forty-year-old. Dressed in tan Dockers and a black polo shirt with the Erie County sheriff's logo on the chest, he looks like the kind of man who would remain anonymous in a crowd if not for the badge pinned to his belt. He is average height, average weight, with dark hair and a rounded nose. His blue eyes, however, disprove the stereotype of an ordinary man. His eyes are curious and inquisitive, the kind that can peer through the superficial and dig deeper to the core of an issue.

It was that ability to detect the unusual that helped capture the Bike Path Rapist.

Patronik took a leading role in the investigation by ensuring that resources were available and that everyone worked within the context of a team. By remaining above the fray of conflicting personalities, he garnered the unwavering respect of his colleagues.

Patronik earned a physics degree from Buffalo State College. He planned to become an engineer, but sat for a

---

[7] Since the case's conclusion, Delano teases Patronik. "I tell him, Ron Kenyon must hate you now," Delano said with a grin. "It was Kenyon's case to begin with, Patronik takes it over, and by the time it's solved, it gets national attention. Scott laughs, and Kenyon is a good guy. I saw him recently and there are no hard feelings."

police exam along with some friends. In 1992, he joined the state police and worked there for five years. He transferred to the sheriff's department and later became a chief.

Realizing the enormity of solving a case that had been open for more than two decades, Patronik rolled up his sleeves and dug in. One of the first things he did was visit the Amherst police station.

"They were in a very cramped space," Patronik said. "Every day there was a standing press conference at 10:00 a.m. that was attended by channels 2, 4, and 7, along with several radio stations."

Patronik believed the daily media briefings were counterproductive. Staged in front of an eight-foot-high granite badge sculpture on the front lawn of Amherst's station, questions kept being steered back to Linda Yalem's unsolved murder. Patronik worried that residents in Clarence and Newstead might think the investigators had lost sight of Joan Diver. Amherst police referenced their national tipline with the phone number (800) BPR-1990. BPR stood for Bike Path Rapist, and 1990 was the year Yalem was murdered.

"This left the impression that Amherst was the only department doing something," Patronik offered. "A few days into it, I objected to daily press conferences. I believed if we had news, then we should inform the media, but not every day."

Amherst wanted to keep the press involved, hoping a break might develop if the case was paraded before the public, so briefings continued.

With Delano working off-site, Patronik's next order of business was to find a new central location where everyone would be comfortable and willing to work. Recognizing space limitations, Amherst had moved the task force office into a bigger conference room, but the root issues remained. With the help of Captain Steve Nigrelli of the state police, Patronik was able to secure space at 45 Oak Street in downtown Buffalo.

Several different county buildings were suggested. Although some were available, there was a time constraint before the space was needed for a different function.

"The question was always, how long do you need it for?" Patronik recalled. "I didn't know. Three months? A year? Three years? This had been an open case for more than twenty years, so there was no timetable on how quickly it would be solved."

The county had recently purchased a vacant building adjacent to the city bus terminal. Because evidence would be stored at the new location, security was essential. By early December, walls were erected to create offices and a conference room, computers were wired for use, and task force members were provided swipe cards to access the building.

But they still needed additional help. The sheriff and Buffalo police sent more people and the state police sent Chris Weber and Betsy Schneider.

Both played pivotal roles behind the scenes. While Weber cleared the growing stack of tips accumulated by the Amherst police, Schneider served as crime analyst. Investigators brought their information to her, and she compiled it to eliminate crossover from officers working in different directions.

At various times during the next several weeks, new members joined the task force. Savage, who had investigated Joan Diver's murder, came on board, as did fellow sheriff's deputy Greg McCarthy.

Task force members had freedom to pursue leads as they saw fit. Each officer would then bring his or her findings back to the group and share. In this manner, everyone contributed important pieces of the puzzle.

"The biggest thing that made the task force work was that people split up to do their own thing," Keats believed. "Chris Weber single-handedly eliminated 150 tips. While we were doing the exciting things, he was doing the mundane work—but it was necessary."

The obstacles of jurisdiction that plagued the task force in Amherst were gone. With a neutral site, the foundation for success was in place. But conflicting personalities continued to be a concern. Patronik worried whether Delano was too abrasive to work with others.

"I had never met Dennis Delano before," Patronik admitted. "My first impression was that I was going to have problems with the guy. He's big and gruff and we took to calling him Sipowicz because he has the same personality as the character from *NYPD Blue*. But that first impression was wrong. Hands down, he's the best cop I've ever seen."

The move to Oak Street on Thursday, December 7, was an important step for the task force. In the new location, everyone was on equal footing and there were no territorial battles to fight.

Removed from the day-to-day conflict, Delano is philosophical about interactions with his colleagues and the relocation to Oak Street.

"All that conflict had a purpose. When I get mad, I'm motivated into working harder. As difficult as that was, everyone who worked the case had talents to contribute. The right personalities rubbed against each other. It wasn't always a happy experience, with arguments and disagreements, but it served a purpose. It all tied together and led to success."

He stood on the dusty pitcher's mound of a softball field behind Frontier High School. It was a windy day, so bystanders raised hoods and thrust hands in pockets, shifting weight from leg to leg. All eyes were on him as he scouted the batter. Winding up, he hurled a pitch over home plate that thwacked into the catcher's mitt.

"Good arm," people muttered.

Wearing the jersey of a local bar, he acknowledged the compliment and scuffed his sneakers, gazing beyond the cyclone fence. Sight lines bumped into thick trees. There were several openings, paths that led into the woods, and he watched kids trek across the lawn before melting into the brush. *What was back there?* he wondered. *Where were they going?*

A few days later, on a summer morning after work, he returned to Hamburg and hiked those trails himself. It was a process of discovery, and what he found intrigued him. One branch of the trail led to Southwestern Boulevard, while another snaked through dense forest. The path splintered off toward a subdivision, but it was largely isolated and secluded. Although there were signs of life surrounding the woods, he could not be spotted from homes or highways. He could remain undetected and see far up and down the trail.

He felt lucky that the softball game had been scheduled there. His reconnaissance had provided him with a new spot. It was time to get out of the city anyway.

He knew if he scouted somewhere, an attack would follow. So on the morning of July 14, 1986, he was lured back to the secrecy of the woods. Jogging through open space, where others could see him, he appeared nondescript. No one noticed him. Once into the foliage, he ducked into undergrowth. Here he lurked, waiting for a victim.

A seventeen-year-old girl appeared shortly before 9:00 a.m. She was by herself, and he had no idea she was late for summer school classes. Seeing her approach, his blood began pounding, and he gazed up and down the path to check they were alone. With great anticipation and a sense of taboo, he burst forth and rushed her from behind.

She knew someone was there, but everything happened quickly. She slowed to allow a runner to pass. Before she could pivot, he coiled the ligature around her neck twice and lifted her from the ground.

He lugged her off the path. Anger seethed. Skin tightened along his jawline. He was master here, fully in control. When her eyes retreated into her skull, he loosened the pressure. It would be no good if she passed out.

"Don't look at my face," he cautioned as consciousness bubbled back. When she uttered a low moan, he told her to shut up. "Take off your clothes and bend over. Have you ever been fucked before?"

Fear swam in her eyes, a sudden numbness and disbelief. *How could this be happening?* Wordlessly, her expression pleaded for mercy, and that aroused him further.

He draped her discarded shirt over her head so vision was impaired. After penetration, he shoved her into a muddy crevice and ordered her to wait twenty minutes before moving.

His heart hammered as he ran from the scene.

First Murder

Once assembled, the task force reviewed case histories in earnest. The last known rape occurred in 1994. New York State's statute of limitations for rape stretched five years, so the clock had expired. The Bike Path Rapist could not be convicted for the myriad attacks in which women survived. But three murders were attributed to him, and there was no stop date for a murder trial. While Diver was the most recent homicide, the initial victim had been killed sixteen years earlier.

Linda Yalem, a twenty-two-year-old UB student, had made plans with her friends to see a movie on the night of Saturday, September 29, 1990. But first she would work out.

Yalem, a communications major, was an avid runner who intended to compete in the New York City Marathon in November, only weeks away. Her training was long-term and intense. Just after noon that Saturday, dressed in black spandex and a white T-shirt that said "Run Like Hell," she left her dorm to do just that along the Ellicott Creek Bike Path. As ducks waded through murky water, Yalem listened to a Tears for Fears cassette while she ran.

The five-mile trail is quiet and picturesque, with wetlands grasses and a meandering creek bordered by thick woods. Cattails spring from the caving banks, dotted with purple and yellow flowers, while insects hum and red-winged blackbirds flit nearby. Metal-framed footbridges arch over streams, horizontal two-by-eight planks echoing when a jogger or bicyclist crosses. The path snakes through the university and continues into Amherst.

Yalem, a native of Thousand Oaks, California, had brown eyes and thick hair to match. She spent the summer of 1990 in her hometown interning at a local newspaper. Buffalo was far from the West Coast, but she chose UB to be near her older sister, Ann Brown, who lived in New York City. Their father had died when Linda was only six. Growing up without a dad, the girls shared a bond, drawn closer by their family's loss. Linda was maid of honor in Ann's wedding. By living in Western New York, Linda could spend semester breaks with her sister, and she planned to camp at Ann's house during the marathon. They had even talked about the meal Linda should eat before embarking on the race—pasta, to be served at Ann's kitchen table.

"I was so proud of her," Brown reflected about her only sister.

The Bike Path Rapist did not know Yalem's name or her history. All he knew was that his urges were intense that Saturday afternoon. The core of darkness was rising, and he burned to find a victim.

This attack, however, would be different. He graduated from rapist to killer.

For a short stretch, the bike path runs loosely parallel to North Forest Road. Before bumping into Dodge
Road, the street dimples toward the paved walkway like
a teardrop, and there is a gravelly shoulder large enough
to park several cars. The bike path is mere steps away.
Beyond a bridge to the left, at mile marker 3.5, foliage
turns dense within a narrow plot of land that separates
the trail from the road.

No one is sure precisely how or when Linda Yalem
was accosted, but her body was found there after 5:00
p.m. the following day.

"He may have parked on North Forest and waited on
the other side of the bridge," LaCorte, the Amherst lieutenant, reflected during a visit to the murder site. "We
don't know if he hid in the bushes or remained visible,
trying to appear non-threatening by leaning down to tie
a shoe. His m.o. was to grab women as they passed by."

The attacker forced a ligature over Yalem's head and
dragged her forty yards on her back along a descending
embankment, stopping in a secluded area with heavy
foliage. It is likely he scouted and pre-selected the spot.

"The trees are so dense that even if someone went
by on the bike path, nothing would be seen," LaCorte
pointed out.

With the garrote firmly in place, concealed by the
underbrush, the attacker took further steps to ensure no
one heard cries for help. He stuck a two-by-five inch strip
of ragged duct tape over her nose, then a second criss-
crossed her mouth, cutting off airways.

When the body was discovered, the T-shirt had been
pulled over her head, and spandex tights and underwear

were bunched around one leg. She was raped and strangled.

"She fought like hell just to breathe," noted Buffalo detective Lissa Redmond after examining photos of the crime scene. "The duct tape covering her nose had been sucked up into her nostrils."

"When I saw those photos, I knew he had no human compassion," Delano reflected in a lowered voice, with reverence that comes from understanding the fragility of life. "While he duct-taped her mouth and nose and strangled her, he had to watch her suffocate. The autopsy report revealed her lungs were congested. That happened because she breathed so hard her blood vessels broke. I've been a cop for a long time, and I believe that every-body is capable of murder. But not too many people are able to watch someone die a slow death. This guy did."

With growing concern, Yalem's roommates con-tacted campus security when she had not returned by 9:30 that night. Friends joined police with flashlights in a hurried probe of the bike path. By 11:30, with a gentle rain falling, they suspended the search until morning.

At sunrise the following day, nearly a dozen officers from Amherst joined fifteen campus police in a more thorough investigation. A helicopter circled above, and bloodhounds pressed noses to the ground, hoping to catch a scent.

Ann Brown was informed of her sister's disap-pearance that Sunday morning. With her husband, she immediately boarded a flight to Buffalo. The best-case scenario was that Linda had hurt herself, was lying wounded just off the bike path, and would be located quickly in daylight. Any other option was too bleak to consider.

At 6:00 p.m., Brown paced in a dorm room with Linda's roommates watching the TV news when an announcement came. A body had been discovered in woods along the bike path. Her sister's friends understood it was Yalem, but Brown remained in denial until a group of officers knocked on the door to make official notification.

"It's like your worst nightmare," Brown recalled years later. "How do I live with knowing what was done to my sister? It still tortures me. Every time I see two sisters together, I feel pain."

The double ligature mark on Yalem's neck suggested the Bike Path Rapist had struck again. But this assault was significantly different, because it was the first time his victim had been killed. In days to come, forensic evidence connected the attacker to the case. Amherst police intensified their efforts, tracking down hundreds of leads, but none panned out.

"He had already done two other rapes in Amherst and we knew that based on m.o.," LaCorte said. "It happened in our community, and we took it personally."

Years later it was learned that the killer had been within their grasp.

A Missed Opportunity

Eleven days after Linda Yalem's murder—on October 9, 1990—Bob McGuire* contacted the Amherst police to report two suspicious incidents around the Ellicott Creek Bike Path. An Amherst resident, McGuire biked along the trail nearly every day before working third shift in a Buffalo factory. Twice within the past fourteen months he had spotted a fellow employee there. The first time he wrote it off as happenstance. But after the second encounter, McGuire started to wonder.

His co-worker, Al Sanchez, also worked night shifts. McGuire reported to police that Sanchez was approximately thirty-five years old, between 5'6" and 5'9", and muscular but not fat. He was Puerto Rican with tan-colored skin.

During the summer of 1989, within days of a fourteen-year-old girl being raped near the bike path, McGuire had noticed Sanchez driving northbound on the 990 highway. He remembered the incident because they had just gotten off shift, and he believed Sanchez lived in Cheektowaga, the opposite direction from which Sanchez was traveling. It was odd to see him in Amherst early in the morning after they had just left work.

Fast forward a year. A few days before the Yalem homicide, on a Wednesday afternoon, McGuire again encountered Sanchez on the bike path, this time near basketball courts by the university. Sanchez caught McGuire's attention because he wore a dark baseball cap with the gold letters "AB-OK." These hats had recently been distributed to American Brass employees. McGuire owned one himself. As he pedaled by, McGuire said hello.

Several days later, McGuire encountered Sanchez at work and asked why he had been on the bike path. His wife was enrolled at UB, Sanchez explained, and he was taking a walk to see her.

These encounters were forgotten until police released a physical description of the Bike Path Rapist. The suspect appeared to resemble Sanchez. McGuire deliberated. Reflecting on their encounters, he knew his co-worker had been in proximity to the path during the time of two attacks. With reservations, McGuire contacted Amherst police.

Investigators ran a background check on Altemio C. Sanchez. He was born January 19, 1958, lived at 76 Allendale Road, Cheektowaga, with his wife, Kathleen, and two sons. He owned two cars—a light blue four-door 1987 Pontiac Grand Am and a 1988 white four-door Pontiac Sunbird. He also owned a Yamaha motorcycle. His previous address was on West Ferry Street in Buffalo. Sanchez had no criminal record.

Police examined cars in the driveway of Sanchez's home. An American Brass sticker was pasted in the left rear window of the Grand Am, and it was noted the car's color and shape matched a witness's description of a vehicle used in a prior assault.

The University at Buffalo had no listing for either Altemio or Kathleen Sanchez. There were four females registered with that surname, but none lived at 76 Allendale Road. Amherst contacted Cheektowaga police to ask if they knew anything about Sanchez, but the name was not familiar, nor was there any record of police calls to his home. It appeared Al Sanchez was a quiet, law-abiding citizen.

On the evening of October 9, 1990, with a steady rain falling, Amherst police set up surveillance on Sanchez's house. At 11:10 p.m., officers had their first glimpse of his round face and mustache. Wearing a baseball cap, dark jacket, and jeans, Sanchez carried a dark duffel bag as he got into his Grand Am and drove toward the highway en route to his job.

Incident reports in the weeks following Yalem's murder reveal the mundane work of chasing leads, most of which did not produce results. The same day McGuire phoned police, for example, Amherst received a call from a woman at Bally Matrix Fitness Center on Robinson Road. A sketch of the killer had been circulated throughout the community, and she noticed someone on the track matching the composite. By the time police arrived at the health club, however, he was gone. Managers recognized the man as a regular member, but did not know his name. They promised to keep a lookout for him and phone authorities the next time he came in.[8]

As other leads were scrutinized, nearly four months went by before Sanchez was revisited as a suspect. While tracking down tips, detectives phoned Sanchez and told

---

[8] Altemio Sanchez did work out at Bally's, but it is unknown if he was the suspect that day. A witness noted the suspicious man got into a red vehicle and drove away. Neither the color of the car nor the partial license number matched anything registered to Sanchez.

him his name had surfaced in an investigation. He agreed to visit the station for an interview the following evening. Sanchez did not ask the nature of the crime in question.

Volunteering to undergo police questioning implies one is innocent. If a man is guilty of a crime—particularly murder—he should flee, not willingly enter into discussions with authorities that hunt him.

Surprisingly, that is not always so.

"It sounds strange, but guilty people often agree to voluntary interviews," Delano explained. "They want to go face to face, sitting down to answer questions, because they're trying to find out how much the police know."

At 7:00 p.m. on January 31, 1991, Sanchez entered the Amherst police station. During a conversation that lasted an hour, he provided background about his life. He moved from Puerto Rico at age two, graduated from Grover Cleveland High School in 1977 and attended Buffalo State College, but never earned a degree. He had owned his home on Allendale Road since 1986. With his wife, Kathleen, he had two boys, ages nine and ten. Prior to moving to Cheektowaga, he lived on Inwood Place in Buffalo, a few blocks from Delaware Park. His mother and stepfather resided in the city, but his father had left home when Sanchez was only two years old. The elder Sanchez was either in Massachusetts or New Jersey.

In the seven years he had worked at American Brass, Sanchez often logged extra hours on the night shift. He gave detectives permission to check with the personnel office there to verify dates and times. The prior summer he dropped off his wife on the Amherst campus for a summer class at UB, but denied ever being on the Ellicott

Creek Bike Path. He was familiar with the activities of the Bike Path Rapist however, because he followed the story in the newspaper.

It is unclear if detectives probed the discrepancies in his testimony. McGuire reported that he encountered Sanchez on the trail; Sanchez claimed he was never there. In addition to working out at Bally Matrix, Sanchez also jogged twice a week in and around Delaware Park.

He signed a waiver, agreeing to submit fingerprint samples and be photographed. The subsequent mug shot shows a balding thirty-three-year-old with dark eyes and a mustache. He appears trim and fit, his youthful face dour, calm but controlled.

At the time, fingerprints were expected to be a key to solving the case.

"There was an abandoned water bottle found near Linda Yalem's body," Patronik explained, having reviewed evidence as part of the task force. "There were fingerprints on the bottle, but no one is sure if the water bottle was used by the rapist. When Amherst interviewed Sanchez, he was fingerprinted, hoping to find a match."

Police soon realized that fingerprints on a water bottle proved little, so they asked suspects to submit DNA samples. But that technology was still primitive in the early 1990s. DNA could be tracked if someone agreed to have blood drawn in a medical laboratory. Results were not returned for up to eight months. Sanchez's DNA was never taken.

American Brass's employee relations office provided investigators with specific dates and times Sanchez was at work. Attacks that were linked to the Bike Path Rapist occurred at 9:35 a.m. on June 12, 1986; at 9:00 a.m. on July 14, 1986; at 8:10 a.m. on June 10, 1988; at 7:45 a.m. on May 1, 1989; at 10:00 a.m. on August 24, 1989; at 8:00 a.m. on May 31, 1990, and just after noon on September 29, 1990. Sanchez was either off shift or vacationing during all the incidents.

While it appeared he had the opportunity, when fingerprint results returned in May, there was no match between those on the water bottle and Sanchez. Because of that, his name was placed on a list of cleared suspects.

"We talked to Sanchez in 1991," LaCorte confirmed. "But every composite of the rapist was drawn with a full head of hair. When we interviewed him he was bald. Whether he wore a wig and confused his victims, we don't know. He had answers for everything, and we didn't suspect him."

Before his arrest, some fellow employees—a father and son working at American Brass—teased him about being the long-sought Bike Path Rapist. They claimed he resembled the dark-eyed man in police sketches that circulated among the community.

"That picture looks just like you," he was told.

Their taunts were meant to be good-natured, but he felt an undercurrent of anxiety. This was scary. The jokes touched too close to the truth, and he had everything to lose.

He tried brushing those men off, steering clear of them and their clique whenever possible. The talk bothered him. It forced him to collide with that other side of himself. Despite his efforts, his cover was only a fragile disguise.

It was a different co-worker, in fact, who alerted the authorities. The closest he came to being caught was when the Amherst police left a message on his answering machine, asking him to come to the station for a voluntary interview.

"They called my house and said they wanted to talk to me," he recalled. It was a terrifying prospect, but to refuse would only raise suspicion.

He knew he was considered a suspect because an American Brass worker had spotted him on the UB bike path. On a summer day, he had walked up and down the pavement while his wife was attending a photography class at the university.

"I know that person who called the Amherst police department," he said years later, remembering little about his fellow employee. "After it happened, we never talked about it at work. I never brought it up to him. His name was Bob something. His last name starts with an L. I can't remember his last name."[9]

At the station, Sanchez was led into a small interview room and fingerprinted. He was scared and tried to

---

[9] Sanchez's recollection is wrong. The man's last name does not begin with the letter "L."

contain his fright, but his body betrayed him. His heart raced; sweat beaded on his forehead. His body shivered with tremors. Officers wondered if he was okay.

"I'm just nervous," he said.

Police described exactly what he had been wearing when his co-worker spotted him on the path. But he denied ever being there, and said that whoever filed the complaint must be mistaken.

"They had me," he admitted. "I was scared I could be arrested for my crimes. I was there for about an hour. They just took my fingerprints and that was it. That was the only time I was called in. I lied to them, obviously. I thought they would call me again, but that never happened."

There is a fine line between a criminal who is caught and one who is able to elude the law. Several key indicators pointed toward Sanchez, but he was one of more than 130 men interviewed.

"The facts of this case slid off their back," Savage reflected of the Amherst police. "Hindsight is twenty-twenty, but if you review Amherst's documents in their entirety, how could they not have gotten him? It's not like the information was from different generations and spread all over the place. It was concise. Everything was there. How could somebody look at that and not connect that this was the guy? You had a co-worker who saw him there. He denied it. You cross-reference that with the dates of the attacks, and he's off the job for every one of them. I can't believe that at a later time, when DNA technology became more reliable, that they didn't try to go back and get a sample from the guy."

"Amherst was right on his tail," Delano said. "They had him, but never asked for a DNA sample. All these years later, nobody can say why. They took his fingerprints, but that wasn't enough. Part of this story is that the system failed, and that's why this guy was allowed to continue preying on women."

As time passed, authorities thought they had the rapist in their sights more than once. But each lead petered out, the promise of a capture dwindling as evidence was gathered. Yalem's murder remained an open file.

"For years, it was the first case our detectives learned about when they came to the bureau," LaCorte said. "At some point, everyone worked on that homicide."

"Our department's policy is that serious cases never go unattended," explained Amherst detective Ed Monan, who was assigned the Yalem file late in 2002. Monan began working for the police department in 1980. He served twenty years in uniform before being promoted to detective in 2000. In his mid-fifties, Monan is tall, with salted hair and a graying mustache. Soft-spoken, his speech comes slowly, as if measuring each word.

"That way there is always one person who is familiar with details of the case should something come up," he said. "The Bike Path case wasn't like others. Many times, there isn't much to do on cold cases, but with that file there were always calls coming in, even ten years later."

Media coverage kept the murder before the public's consciousness. Newspapers and TV stations revisited the unsolved rapes and murder regularly. The Amherst police knew when the episode from *America's Most Wanted* was replayed because of the bump in tips that followed.

Throughout Western New York, the name Linda Yalem became synonymous with safety precautions. The University at Buffalo held an annual race each fall to honor her memory. The message of the Linda Yalem Memorial Run stressed that individuals practice caution when exercising outdoors, without letting fear prevent anyone from using a bike path. Approximately 1,500 runners participated annually.

During the 1996 race, held six years to the day after Yalem's murder, Al Sanchez registered under his own name, was assigned race number 679, and participated in the 3.1-mile run.

"A bunch of guys from work put together a running club," he recalled. "They asked me if I wanted to do the Linda Yalem run. I don't know what made me do it, but yes, I ran that race. It crossed my mind what I had done to her."

Second Murder

He repeated the name only when it was spoken to him first. "Majane Mazur, yeah," he mumbled. It is unclear whether he ever knew her last name while she was alive.

Meeting her was a fluke. On a day when he got out of work earlier than expected, he was driving along Kensington Avenue en route home. He saw a redhead stepping out of a car. Clearly, she was a prostitute. He honked the horn, veered toward her, and made contact.

Not tonight, he said, but maybe sometime we could have a date. She scratched a phone number onto a scrap of paper and slipped it through his rolled-down window. A few days later he called. At a curb in front of the Huron Hotel, she plopped in the passenger's seat and they drove to Exchange Street.

"At first, I didn't have any intent to kill her. I picked her up, gave her $40, and we had sex in the backseat. What made me kill her, I don't know. Anger and excitement started to build at the same time. I stuck a bag over her head while we were having sex. She never knew I had the rope in my pocket."

Small but spirited, she began to protest, pulling away and fighting him. If he let go, she would tell that he had forced a plastic bag over her head. She knew his face.

She could describe his car. That information would lead authorities directly to him because of previous ligature attacks.

He was committed now.

"Once we had sex, I took the rope out and put it around her neck and strangled her. She didn't say anything to me. I could have got up and put my pants on and she could have done the same. I don't know what made me click. You don't just go around strangling people, but I did. I had the chance to do the same thing to other people. Why did I start? I don't know why."

Without pause, his recollections came to a close. "I took her body, put it in a field, and left."

Bad people sometimes get away with murder. For many years it appeared Majane Mazur's killer would not be caught. The 1992 death was charted by the city as an unsolved homicide and the case grew cold as time passed. Late in 2004, however, some dozen years after the body's discovery, DNA analysis revealed a shocking truth: The Bike Path Rapist was responsible.

The attack on Mazur did not fit neatly into the rapist's previous profile. She differed from other victims in several ways. She knew the killer and had contact with him beforehand. Working as a prostitute, he solicited her for sex at least one other time before her death. This did not match his pattern of attacking random women. She was killed in a car, not along a secluded path, and the body was dragged to an open field where it was crudely covered. A plastic bag was twisted over her head, sealed below the chin until she suffocated.

A petite redhead, the thirty-two-year-old Mazur was last seen getting into a four-door white Pontiac Sunbird after 11:00 p.m. on October 30 outside her apartment on Huron Street. Likely the homicide occurred that night, but the specific day and time of her death are unknown. Mazur's boyfriend, Alberto Turner,* knew she was going on a "date," and told police that as he watched through an apartment window, he saw the man's hand reach to unlock the passenger's door. The skin appeared white, he said, but Turner never saw the driver's face. After two days, when Mazur did not return home, he filed a missing person's report.

Unlike Linda Yalem, and later, Joan Diver, the murder did not receive a spate of media attention. It was convenient to write this death off. Mazur worked as a prostitute, after all, and was a crack user. Near the end of her life, she existed on the fringes of society, having already left a husband and four-year-old daughter to fend for themselves in a community south of Buffalo while she took an apartment in Buffalo.

Her story did not begin that way. Born Majane Elizabeth Phillips, she grew up in Greenville, South Carolina, part of a successful upper-class family. Her grandfather had been mayor, and as a child, she took dance lessons and rode horses. In college, she used drugs recreationally. But her introduction to crack caused a rapid downward spiral.

At the time of her death, Mazur's life was gripped by addiction, and she struggled day to day for basic necessities. Often lacking funds, she accepted money from unlikely sources. She had only recently begun prostituting herself.

A fifty-one-year-old man from Dunkirk had befriended Mazur and regularly wired cash for groceries and rent. He denied there was a sexual element to their relationship. Although she and her husband had one daughter, Mazur became pregnant with another man's child. Six weeks before her death, she gave that baby up for adoption, for which she was paid $13,000. Turner, with whom she lived, was also a recovering drug user whom she met during a rehab stint at Sheehan Memorial Hospital in the summer of 1992. He described himself as her boyfriend, but police wondered about the scope of their relationship.

"Majane was a pretty girl and a college graduate, but she got hooked on crack," Delano said. "Coming out of rehab, she wound up at the Huron Hotel. At the time, rooms were rented as efficiency apartments. She lived there with her boyfriend, a black guy named Alberto Turner. There's some question whether he was her pimp, but she called him her boyfriend."

Following the discovery of Mazur's body, police interviewed Turner. He said that on the day she disappeared, a john called the apartment around 4:00 p.m. and spoke to his girlfriend, requesting a date for that evening. The man was familiar with Mazur, having hired her before. Turner knew nothing about him, except Mazur mentioned in passing that he liked bowling.

"In 1991, Sanchez had been arrested for picking up an undercover police officer," Delano noted. "After he was popped, he decided he wasn't going to solicit girls off the street anymore. For a while, he only used prostitutes that he knew. He had Majane's phone number from a prior encounter."

After she vanished, Mazur's husband trekked to Buffalo from his home in Dunkirk to pick up her clothes and personal belongings. Police investigated the disappearance, wondering if Mazur had enemies or experienced conflicts with any customers. They searched for suspects driving a white Pontiac Sunbird, and found a man whose vehicle matched that description. He even admitted to frequenting prostitutes. Excitement was tempered when he confessed he was gay and only hired males.

Fellow hookers turned police onto a customer who was known to pay for sex, then turn abusive once the act was finished. He would choke the girl, hold a knife to her throat, demand his money back, and shove her out of the car before speeding away. Other prostitutes talked nervously about a ring of Mexicans trolling through Buffalo and Rochester who hired hookers to star in porn films. Desperate for drug money, the girls agreed to be paid $500 for fifteen or twenty minutes of filmed sex. Women were frightened, however, by rumors that these were actually snuff films, in which a girl was killed on camera.

Although police investigated, none of these leads could be connected to Mazur. For three weeks, she vanished completely.

Before noon on Sunday, November 22, 1992, a middle-aged farmer from Amherst and his two teenage sons scouted a field around railroad tracks parallel to Exchange Street in downtown Buffalo. The man was a flower dealer, and he and his boys searched for unique specimens.

The farmer encountered a bundle lying on the ground, and noticed what appeared to be a human head protruding from beneath a plastic cover. Using his foot to pry back the corrugated board, he was shocked to discover a decomposing body lying face down. Dashing to the nearby Amtrak station, he phoned police, informing them of his grisly find.

Authorities examined the surrounding area and found a condom wrapper, sneaker, and sock. Two plastic bags—one white, the other black—were wrapped around the woman's head, while a pair of fiberglass panels covered the scene.

The medical examiner noted that pants were bunched around the victim's right leg and she appeared to have been dragged on her back. By studying decomposition, it was estimated the body had been there for one to two weeks. There were bite marks on one leg, likely from a rat or other animal.

"She was raped," Delano observed. "She wasn't strangled so much as suffocated with a plastic bag over her head. Like Yalem, it's clear with this case that he watched her die."

After Yalem's murder, the killer made no effort to hide the body, perhaps because it was a secluded location. The only attempt to camouflage Diver was to drape her fleece jacket across her sternum, yet that was a densely wooded area as well. Mazur's body, however, was discovered in an open field, which may explain the concerted effort to cover her with stray remnants of garbage.

"Because of the way he positioned her, we did question whether he experimented with returning periodi-
cally to check on the body," Delano recalled. "With the
other murders, he didn't care. But with this one he put a
piece of fiberglass over her, some rocks on top, a garbage
bag. We don't know why. There are cases where guys
sometimes go back and revisit their victims. I don't know
if that happened here, but it may have. She wasn't found
for several weeks."

The 2004 revelation of a DNA link to the Bike Path
Rapist rekindled interest in Mazur's cold case and altered
the investigation's focus. If the notorious attacker had
killed a prostitute that no one had previously connected
to him, could there be other unsolved murders for which
he was responsible?

Attack survivors had provided descriptions of the Bike
Path Rapist that evolved over the years, and composite
sketches had been circulated. It was agreed the killer
had a Mediterranean look, with dark eyes and a round
face. Often his head was covered with a baseball cap or a
knit hat. But when tracking a criminal, witness descriptions are only part of the equation. Such testimony is an
imperfect science, because of the short span of time that
the victim sees her attacker and the psychological trauma
that rape inflicts.

"I don't mean for this to come out sounding callous,"
Delano said. "But rape victims rarely get a good look at
their attacker. I don't care what they say. We've heard

women swear *I know it's him*. But you're talking about less than a minute looking at a guy's face under extremely emotional conditions. Can they positively say that's the guy who raped me? Look at a guy long enough, and she can convince herself it's him. There is a strong desire, naturally, to accuse somebody of the crime because a victim is so internally troubled by what happened. Before this case, I didn't understand that victim IDs aren't always reliable."

When the Bike Path Rapist was most active during the 1980s, eyewitness recollections were the strongest leads offered to investigators. Sometimes—with no malice intended—that information was wrong.

DNA analysis came into widespread use in the 1990s and has revolutionized police work. Because of its statistical accuracy, uncertainty has been removed. Using DNA results, scientists can compare markers left at a crime scene with that of a suspect. Profiling techniques have advanced dramatically as well, offering another pillar to support an investigation.

Profiling is a controversial method for tracking a criminal. In spite of the slick, glamorous profession depicted on TV dramas, some police are skeptical of its effectiveness. There is a debate over how profiling should best be used. Can it provide definitive answers or simply offer a hazy outline that hints at facts?

"The problem with profilers is that you give them specifics and they feed you back generalities," said Amherst detective Ed Monan.

With their only goal to capture the serial killer, members of the task force were willing to accept help from any credible source. The FBI's Behavioral Science Unit is considered the premier collection of profilers throughout the world. A team visited Buffalo from its base in Quantico, Virginia, to analyze the case. The Bike Path Rapist had been on the FBI's radar during the litany of attacks in the 1980s and 1990s, but after a dozen years of silence, the profile needed to be updated. Profiling techniques had changed greatly in the past ten years.

"In retrospect, it's impressive how much they got right," Patronik said. "They told us three key things, all of which proved true."

When the investigation began, the Bike Path Rapist's first known attack was in Delaware Park in 1986. It was well organized and executed with confidence. Because of that, profilers did not believe it was his first attempt. It was suspected he had committed earlier rapes. Mazur, the homicide victim in 1992, worked as a prostitute, so profilers reasoned that was not a coincidence and the killer likely had some tie-in with prostitutes. The third thing they suggested was to not become overly focused on the weapon. He may have used different weapons at different times. In fact, in some early rapes he used a gun or a knife and then changed to the ligature.

"After the FBI updated the profile, they drew a circle on the west side of Buffalo," recalled Greg Savage. "Some of the early rapes occurred there. They weren't sure about the exact connection, but insisted there was a link to that area. Time proved that they were right on the money."

The profile provided a springboard toward honing in on suspects, but it was DNA analysis that narrowed the investigative focus.

A DNA print processed in 2004 analyzed the Bike Path Rapist's ancestry. Statistically, he was 51 percent European, 30 percent Native American, 13 percent Sub-Saharan African, and 6 percent East Asian.

"With this genealogy breakdown, everyone assumed he was Native American," Delano said. "That conclusion struck me as wrong. It didn't make sense for him to be Indian. Many of the rapes took place near Delaware Park. You don't see Indians jogging there."

On December 4, 2006, three days before the move to Oak Street, Dr. John Simich of the Erie County Central Police Services Crime Lab addressed the task force, giving officers a crash course on the science of DNA. Techniques could be employed to find a suspect or eliminate one. Based on percentages, he was able to suggest what physical attributes the killer should have.

"Dr. Simich created an ethnicity profile," Patronik recalled. "There was no guarantee, but statistically, the sum of the parts suggested we would be looking for a Hispanic or a South American, probably from Colombia."

Delano said that presentation helped clear up any misconceptions about the rapist's ethnic makeup. "It was explained that everybody who had this combination of percentages is Hispanic. That profile, with those numbers, represents a Hispanic male. Nobody put that together until he told us."

DNA evidence proved a key to solving the crime and saying with certainty that the right man was caught. Members of the task force re-aligned their search, trying to narrow the focus onto Hispanics, because the DNA marker Simich identified had been passed paternally.

But this approach was not foolproof. Other avenues still needed to be pursued.

"It wouldn't be 100 percent accurate," Josh Keats cautioned. "Suppose the killer had been adopted and had a different ethnic last name? In my opinion, however, that was our best chance at that point in the investigation."

Keats and Betsy Schneider spent most of Friday, December 22, at the Amherst Police Department, combing through extensive files. While re-reading reports about long-ago rapes and Linda Yalem's murder, a list was compiled of all Spanish surnames they encountered.

"We went through every Hispanic name that was referenced, even if it was just someone who called in a tip," Keats said. "Once that was done, I had to figure out if the person was eliminated as a suspect, and see if the investigation that cleared him was solid. You can't rely completely on past police work because the bad guy is still out there."

Keats worked forward from "A," and Schneider began at the end of the alphabet, reading backwards from "Z." Many of the recorded names were ruled out quickly, but by day's end a significant list was assembled.

One person on the list was Altemio Sanchez. He did not leap out at investigators however, which is understandable considering that other references to him were buried in old files along with hundreds of unfamiliar suspects.

Schneider typed all the information into a spreadsheet, which was melded against names of men who had been arrested for soliciting prostitutes in the past decade. Ten Hispanics fit the profile, falling in the correct

age range and having a connection to one or more of the
rape locations. Keats's plan was to track down each and
secure a DNA sample.

The Chart

In the days following his self-imposed exile from the
Amherst police station, before the task force assembled
at Oak Street, Dennis Delano worked at his desk in downtown Buffalo. He and Alan Rozansky were in frequent
contact, so Delano was informed of daily developments.

Using copies made from the Amherst police files,
he read about the three homicides. While familiarizing
himself with the murders, he considered new angles to
study. He then began combing through old rape cases.

Detective Lissa Redmond, from the Sex Crimes
unit, was not officially part of the task force yet, but was
familiar with the probe because she had investigated the
last known rape that occurred in 1994. Delano sought
her help finding that paperwork. The files were stored at
headquarters, on the same floor and around the corner
from the cold case office.

Delano went through boxes and pulled folders that
he thought were related. Attacks before 1986 were in a
separate file from those after 1986.

"When I read them there were too many similarities
to ignore," Delano said. "I kept reviewing the statements,
but I couldn't mentally get a grasp on all the information,
so I started laying it out side by side. Once I was able to
see it, that's when it started making sense."

Once the office at Oak Street opened, Delano
trudged in with files and stacked them on a wheeled cart.

Using an eleven by fourteen–inch piece of card stock, he laid out a rudimentary table listing attacks done by the Bike Path Rapist and similar rapes that fit the profile. A more complete chart, with contributions from others, later replaced this first draft.

The grid was organized into columns listing chronological years, with fifteen entries from 1981 to 1994. Fourteen rows labeled year, date, victims' names, victims' ages, general location of attack, specific location, time, method of rapist's approach, attack position, weapon, how the victim's clothes were removed, position of the rape, how long the victim was instructed to wait until seeking help, and physical descriptions of the attacker.

Converting this complex data into graphic form allowed detectives to see a visual representation of evil spanning a long block of time. It suggested that the Bike Path Rapist was far more active than anyone had previously considered.

The revised chart illuminated several interesting facts. With information from twenty-one attacks laid out side by side, a profile emerged spanning from May 1977 to his last known attack in October 1994 before he resumed with the Diver homicide.

• In six of the first nine assaults, his weapon of choice was a gun.[10] Beginning in 1985, he switched to a

---

[10] In a November 2007 jailhouse interview, Sanchez claimed he only used a gun once, but it was a pellet gun. Six different victims contradict that, however, claiming they were accosted by a man with a handgun. DNA evidence linked Sanchez to three of those victims.

ligature, using it exclusively from then on with two exceptions: In a 1986 rape he used a knife and in a 1989 attempted rape he wrapped his hands around the victim's neck from behind.

• The turning point came in 1984. During an attack on a staircase leading to a railroad overpass along Delaware Avenue, he set his gun on the steps while fondling the victim. Although her face was covered with a knit cap pulled down over her eyes, she could see through a narrow seam where fabric arched over the bridge of her nose. Thinking quickly, the twenty-year-old victim grabbed the pistol, bashing his head with the handle.

"He got very mad," the woman later recalled before a grand jury. "He grabbed my hair and said, that was a really stupid thing to do, bitch, and that he's killed girls before and that he would kill me."

Rapist and victim each vied for control of the gun, struggling loudly.

"After I hit him, he grabbed me," the woman recalled. "We both had our hands on the gun, and we kept going back and forth, pointing it at my chest and pointing away. And I was screaming. That's the only time I was screaming. Finally I realized I wasn't going to win, this gun could go off, and I pushed it at him and pushed it away."

Safely in control again, the assault quickly escalated from fondling to rape.

Although he used a handgun once more in an attack three months later, detectives believe this incident was the key motivation for switching to a ligature.

"With every new attack, a rapist learns something and modifies his behavior next time," Delano noted.

"After the gun was taken away from him, he probably said to himself, screw this," Rozansky reflected. "He didn't want to get killed, so he went with a different method."

• Before 1985, there was no preferred time of attack. Hours vary: 1:30 a.m., 9:30 a.m., 5:00 p.m., 10:50 p.m. Beginning in 1986, all assaults occurred in the early morning, between 7:00 a.m. and noon.[11]

• Three times he used the name "Dave" when talking to his victims. In 1977 and 1989 he said, "My name is Dave." In 1985, during the assault of a prostitute, he told her, "My name is Al Davis." This phrase may have originated from his familiarity with a replica of Michelangelo's statue of David in Delaware Park, where several rapes occurred, although each of the three attacks where he said this took place outside of the park.

• In the four years between 1983 and 1986, there were three attacks each year, except for 1985, when there was only one. 1989 also had three attacks—two rapes and one unsuccessful attempt.

---

[11] Around this time, Sanchez began working third shift at American Brass. By staggering their schedules, either he or his wife could be home with the boys and avoid shuffling them to day care.

"This tells me we're probably missing two rapes from 1985," Delano noted, pointing out a break in the pattern. "I wonder how many more of these he did that were never reported. Many of his victims were college students because he operated around Buffalo State."

- In the unsuccessful attempt in 1989, a twenty-two-year-old student was sunbathing in Delaware Park. Grabbed from behind, her bikini bottom was ripped off, but she struggled enough to escape. Once his fingers slipped from her neck, the attacker ran into the woods.

- Delano noted the rapist lurked in the woods waiting for the right time to emerge.

   "If the opportunity was there, he'd rape a girl," Delano said. "He'd been exposing himself in Delaware Park and got away with it every time."

- He ordered victims not to look at him, often giving the woman something to cover her eyes. Twice he removed a knit cap from his own head, placed it on the victim, and pulled it down to the tip of her nose, limiting her vision to a shadowy silhouette. Twice he produced a tube top, ordering the woman to shield her face with it. Two other times he yanked off the victim's shorts and used them to cover her head. By 1986, rather than shorts, women were ordered to use their shirts as a blinder. Beginning in 1988, he used duct tape to cover his victims' eyes and mouth.

* The time he ordered his victims to wait after an assault also grew as years passed. In a 1981 rape, he told the victim, "Give me thirty seconds." The next attack, in 1983, increased to five minutes. After that, the wait time expanded to ten, then twenty minutes. By 1989, a fourteen-year-old was told, "give me forty minutes." Several victims complied with the long interlude. Because their eyes were covered, they were unsure if he still waited nearby, and took no chance of further angering him.

* Joan Diver and a 1986 rape victim were over forty years old, while Majane Mazur and two other victims were in their early thirties. But he primarily targeted teenagers and women in their twenties. Twice he assaulted fourteen-year-old girls. There were also victims age fifteen, sixteen, seventeen, and nineteen.

Once the chart had been drafted, the next step was to use the conference room's white board to expand the analysis. Delano, Josh Keats, and state police captain Steve Nigrelli rolled a cart of files into the common area and began combing files. Using a dry-erase marker, Nigrelli sketched out a wall-sized table.

"As Steve was listing the cases on the board, we realized that so many of them matched," Delano recalled. "People coming in were saying, *Holy shit, this guy must have done these rapes too.* Now we could take a different angle because if we caught someone for the later rapes, we could pin the early ones on him."

Many unsolved assaults were quickly ruled out because certain characteristics did not match. A cluster of attacks happened near Buffalo State College and Delaware Park, so a rapist working on Buffalo's west side was near the target location, but was identified as African-American. Details had to fall in line with prior descriptions and methods.

As the chart swelled with similarities, Greg Savage wandered into the conference room and studied the list. He recognized two rapes that had already been cleared. Twenty years earlier, he had worked as a guard at the Erie County Holding Center. A prisoner there, Anthony Capozzi, was indicted for three rapes occurring in 1985, and was convicted in January 1987 for two.

This was news to Delano and the team, because nothing in the files indicated any of these cases had been solved.

"My first year on the job I worked in the jail," Savage recalled. "That was right after Capozzi had been arrested. He was on the block and I dealt with him every day. I knew that he was convicted as the Delaware Park rapist."

In fact, Capozzi was still locked up in Attica State Prison. But when all the facts were displayed on the chart, something was not right.

Perhaps Capozzi had committed the growing list of rapes prior to 1985. But the attacks continued in the same location, even after Capozzi was jailed.[12] The Bike Path Rapist was already linked to assaults in Delaware Park in 1981 and 1986. But the similarities with later attacks were too distinct to ignore. Each rapist had approached the victim from the front, passed, then attacked from

behind. Each told the woman to wait ten minutes after
he left. Was there a copycat at work?

How could Capozzi be the elusive rapist and killer,
active since 1985, if he had been jailed for more than
twenty-one years?

There was also the issue of Capozzi's mental health.
Nearly thirty years earlier, he had been diagnosed as
schizophrenic. Savage's recollection from the 1980s was
that he was disturbed.

"Back then he was sick. He'd sit in his bunk all night,
rocking and staring at the wall," Savage reflected. "It
seemed to me he wasn't capable of hardcore rapes. But I
was just a twenty-six-year-old kid who never hung out in

---

[12] In a memorandum dated July 11, 1986, the district attorney's office argued
that a later rape was irrelevant because victims of earlier assaults were able to
positively identify Anthony Capozzi as the rapist, and the methods of operation
in each attack were identical.

The DA's office suggested the defense might wish to introduce a June
12, 1986 rape as evidence, although "there is no substantial or concrete proof
that the man who is responsible for the attacks on the three victims for which
the defendant is being tried is the same man who is responsible for the attack
on June 12, 1986. On the contrary, the attack on June 12, 1986 is quite dissim-
ilar in that this rape occurred some two years after the original series of rapes;
the attacker, in the recent incident, used tremendous physical force nearly
sending the victim into a state of unconsciousness unlike the other attacks;
the physical description given in the latter is significantly different as well…
the location of all the rapes in question occurred in the Delaware Park area.
However, it is not uncommon for a rape to occur in the Park. In fact, numerous
rapes and attacks have occurred in the area especially during the spring/sum-
mer months. Further, in all four attacks the attacker made the victim wait ten
minutes as well as shielding their faces from his appearance. This certainly
may well have been nothing more than a mere coincidence."

Delano, who reached a different conclusion more than twenty years later,
was disgusted after reading the memo. "They played these little games, and an
innocent man went to jail. I try to make sense of it, but it's sickening."

the city, so what did I know? I remember thinking sarcastically, *This is the mastermind Delaware Park rapist?*"

As the task force poured over files, it became evident that the rapist was methodical and cunning. He pre-scouted locations, cleared areas of foliage where assaults were committed, and laid out strips in advance to tape a victim's mouth. The rapist was detailed in his approach.

"We had rapes from the early 80s, then the ones Capozzi was accused of, then more after that, and they all occurred in the same spot," Savage summarized. "We suspected these rapes were done by the same person. Evidence showed us it had to be the same guy."

Back in 1985, two separate witnesses identified Capozzi in a lineup, certain he was the man responsible for the rapes. Their testimony cemented his conviction. There was no DNA or other evidence to link him. Was it possible that the wrong man had been jailed?

"We studied the board and discussed possibilities," Rozansky recalled. "Finally, we said, enough is enough. How long are we going to look at this? Let's take a ride to Attica and talk to Capozzi."

Anthony Capozzi

Attica State Prison is notorious for the 1971 riots, in which a five-day mutiny claimed thirty-nine lives, including ten correctional officers. Nearly forty years later, it remains an intimidating place. Surrounded by smooth stone walls, the prison is a nearly impregnable fortress that houses New York State's most nefarious criminals. Once inside, visitors feel tremendous tension in the air. One misplaced glance could ignite a firestorm.

Police officers wishing to visit an inmate must contact the Inspector General's office in Albany ahead of time. A meeting is scheduled for a specific hour, and anyone entering the prison—even cops—must undergo extensive security checks coming in and out.

"Attica is the real deal," Greg Savage noted ominously. "It's a serious place."

Four days before Christmas, Savage, Alan Rozansky, and Scott Patronik, traveled an hour east to meet with fifty-year-old Anthony Capozzi.[13] The native of Buffalo's

---

[13] Although Delano was a driving force behind the efforts to free Capozzi, he was not present at this initial meeting. "Patronik and Rozansky snookered me on that one," he chuckled. "They visited Attica on my day off. They called me at home before they left. I asked them to wait twenty-four hours so I could join them, but they didn't."

west side had been incarcerated since his arrest in 1985, but he and his family had steadfastly maintained his innocence.

A short, burly man with dark hair and a distant smile, Capozzi first experienced symptoms of schizophrenia after high school. He became delusional, seeing faces and hearing voices. He believed the television talked to him. Struggling to make it through each day, Capozzi held no job and lived with his parents, who felt powerless about the change in their son's personality. It was not unusual for Capozzi to spend his days wandering the city sidewalks. Leaving the family home on Jersey Street, he walked for miles to visit two sisters, one on Parkside Avenue and the other near Sterling Avenue in north Buffalo.

A citizen's report of a suspicious man led authorities to consider him a suspect in the Delaware Park rapes. Because of his illness, he exhibited bizarre behavior. He also matched witness descriptions.

At 10:00 p.m. on September 12, 1985, four detectives visited Capozzi's home, searching for clothing and a weapon. Although nothing was found, the following morning officers woke Capozzi and took him into custody.

Although his mother wept, Anthony told her, "Don't worry, Mom. I'll be back."

But he never came back.

At Attica, Capozzi was led into a room and took his place across a table from the three investigators. Rozansky was the first to speak.

"Anthony, did you ever go to Delaware Park?"

"I go . . . I go . . . I go to Delaware Park," Capozzi answered softly, short hair now peppered with gray, the stuttering a facet of his everyday speech.

"Did you ever hurt anybody there?"

"I . . . I . . . I didn't hurt anybody. I . . . I . . . I play Frisbee at Delaware Park."

Rozansky sought to build rapport, suggesting they should play Frisbee together some time in the future.

"I was just saying that out of the goodness of my heart," Rozansky noted. "I didn't really believe it. We were there to pick his brain, thinking it would help our case."

Within minutes, it was clear to the detectives that this man was not connected to the Bike Path Rapist. They also had second thoughts about whether he committed the rapes in Delaware Park for which he was convicted.

"I hadn't seen Capozzi in twenty years," Savage said. "But as we started to investigate him, we had a feeling this guy could be innocent. When we met him at Attica, he could hold a conversation, but you can tell he's out of it. Some of the things he says are off the wall."

Capozzi told the officers some of his fellow inmates were nine hundred years old. Despite the fact that he was talking to policemen who might aid in his exoneration, Capozzi grew anxious to end the interview. "Are we about done here, guys?" he asked. "I . . . I . . . I have to go. It's spaghetti night in the cafeteria."

"He's such a simple guy," Savage acknowledged. "He's like a kid. You get the feeling he's not capable of lying."

Parole had been refused to him five times because he would not admit wrongdoing.

"Oh no," Capozzi insisted. "I . . . I . . . I would never rape a woman. I have three sisters. My parents raised me right. I . . . I . . . I would never do that. I truly am an innocent man."

It is not unusual for a prisoner to lament his innocence—but Capozzi was different. Veteran cops, hardened from years of dealing with criminals, considered the possibility that he was telling the truth.

"His protests were the most lucid thing he was saying," Savage recalled. "He has severe emotional problems but as disturbed as he is, he's believable. We came out and all three of us thought he got hung out for something he didn't do."

"I said to my partners, 'Do you think for one minute that this guy's capable of these crimes?'" Rozansky said. "The rapist was cunning. He scouted locations. He laid out strips of tape in advance and ran up behind a victim to cover her head with a bag. Capozzi wasn't able to think that way. When we left Attica, I was blinking away tears. I knew he had never hurt anybody."

The task force had unearthed information that pointed in a new direction. Their charge was to capture a serial killer, but what should they do after discovering the wrong man had been jailed? It was unfamiliar territory for veteran cops, and it gnawed at their conscience.

"I was waking up in the middle of the night knowing that guy was sleeping in a little cell," Delano said, passion permeating his voice. "He doesn't belong there, and he has a mental condition, which makes it even worse."

Support for Capozzi's innocence received a boost a week later, near the end of December, when six task force members braved the winter weather and traveled to old crime scenes. The goal was to assemble a geographic profile. Doing this effectively was a challenge because in twenty-plus years since the assaults, landscapes had been altered. Buildings had been erected and trees felled. Because of the rapes, much of the brush had been cleared in Buffalo's Delaware Park, leaving the area more open. Working from old photos and trying to account for changes like foliage growth and removal, the various officers began at separate locations. By identifying tree trunks, the different teams converged at one spot, east of the statue of David in Delaware Park. All agreed that the same patch, only a few square yards, was where several different rapes occurred.

"Now we were really convinced," Patronik said. "What are the odds that Capozzi did two rapes here and the Bike Path Rapist did the others in the same spot? We believed the Bike Path Rapist did the rapes Capozzi was accused of."

The task force was not ready to go public with cries of Capozzi's innocence, however. Instead, Rozansky requested files of the case from Capozzi's lawyer and the district attorney's office. Neither understood why those old cardboard crates would have any bearing on the hunt for a serial rapist, and task force members were keeping quiet.

Rozansky repeatedly phoned Thomas D'Agostino, Capozzi's attorney. But when he could not be reached, Rozansky refused to leave a detailed message, because he did not want the lawyer to think he was trying to link Capozzi to additional crimes or incriminate him further. Although Rozansky was unable to make contact, Delano did.

Delano was steamed because the system had failed. As he reviewed files from two decades earlier, he was amazed that no one recognized Capozzi's innocence.

"I'm a homicide investigator," he said. "I know the homicides that have occurred in the last few years. If you mention them to me, I'm familiar with the names. In the mid-80s, Buffalo police formed the Sex Offense Squad. They worked rapes and assaults exclusively. Somebody back then should have known the rapes before and after Capozzi's arrest were exactly the same. It boggles my mind that no one saw a relation. Meanwhile, Anthony Capozzi is sitting in jail.

"After I made the chart, it was obvious this couldn't be two different people. Either the rapist is the same person, who's Capozzi, or it's somebody else. It can't be Capozzi because he's in prison. How did so many people look the other way on this?"

Delano wrote e-mails to the parole board and the governor in which he shared the group's findings and wondered what could be done about an innocent man's plight. He maintained that there was a strong element of doubt, so at minimum, Capozzi should be granted parole.

But justice plodded too slowly for Delano's liking. Frustrated, he realized that no one was anxious to investigate a prior conviction. Many of the key players in Capozzi's 1987 trial had become respected names in the legal community. Twenty years earlier, Frank Clark was not yet elected to his position as Erie County District Attorney, but he did work in the office. One of Delano's fellow Buffalo detectives had assembled evidence, and the assistant district attorney who prosecuted the case, Sheila DiTullio, was now an Erie County judge. Richard Arcara, who had been district attorney then, was now a federal judge. It would be embarrassing for prominent people if a decades-old wrongful conviction came to light. This crusade was to be an unpopular one.

"I wasn't winning any friends, that's for sure," Delano chuckled.

Still, it was logical that Delano voice the injustice. He had the full support of his boss, chief of detectives Dennis Richards, and jurisdiction, because the Buffalo police had arrested Capozzi years ago. Other people's careers hung in the balance. Some task force members needed to contribute ten or twenty more years to the job before they could retire. If there was political backlash, Delano could walk away any time. In fact, he had planned to retire before being called back to capture the Bike Path Rapist.

"What was the worst thing that could happen to me?" Delano wondered rhetorically. "They could bump me back to homicide. Okay, fine. I'd love to work there, too. I had nothing to lose. Besides, if doing the right thing cost me my job, I'd find another job. I'd rather pump gas somewhere than know I contributed to an innocent man sitting in jail."

Some of Delano's colleagues remained silent about the Capozzi situation, perhaps considering it a distraction from their primary purpose. Others believed lobbying on his behalf was a fool's errand, because DNA was the sole method to prove innocence, and it did not appear that any DNA evidence from the Capozzi cases still existed.

"Someone said to me, '*if* Capozzi is innocent,'" Delano recalled. "I said, what do you mean, *if?* Look at the chart! The evidence is right there!"

On the white board in his Oak Street office, Delano organized his priorities for the investigation. Number one on the list, printed in black marker, was "Free Capozzi."

A Buried File

For most people, Friday afternoon signals the end of work. But the men and women on the task force understood their jobs had no parameters. Time was elastic, its boundaries flexible. So long as a killer lurked in the shadows, they remained involved with the investigation, working whenever new leads developed, regardless of the clock.

Transcripts from the Capozzi trial arrived at the command center on Friday, January 5, 2007. In the depths of winter, darkness fell early. As afternoon waned, Scott Patronik remained at his desk while his colleagues filtered out. Patronik felt divided. His wife wanted him home, and he was anxious to play with their new baby. The Capozzi files, however, were intriguing. It had taken several days of maneuvering, prodding, and calls back and forth, but finally they were here. He phoned his wife to say he would be delayed, then spread the manila folders across his desk. Opening the one on top, he examined each piece of paper methodically.

"Time flew as I was reading," Patronik said. "It took a while to piece it all together because the file was disorganized."

A mimeographed eight-and-a-half by fourteen sheet, creased at the bottom so it would fit in a folder, contained the blurred font of a statement given by a twenty-one-year-old student. Written the day after she was raped while walking toward Buffalo State College, Patronik read her recollections from nearly twenty-six years ago:

At about 9:45 a.m. yesterday, 4/14/81, I was walking through Delaware Park on my way to school and was just about at the Statue of David area when I passed a jogger running in the opposite direction. I didn't think anything of it because I see joggers in the park all the time, although that morning was a rainy day and he was really the only one I saw.

I kept on walking when all of a sudden this same guy came up behind me and as I turned to see who it was he grabbed me by the front of my coat at the collar. I started to hit him with my umbrella and that's when he showed me this knife. It was like a scalpel but larger. It had a light brown handle, I believe, and the blade didn't look shiny and was about three inches long and curved at the end.

He said, "Come with me or I'll cut your fuckin' face." He kept pulling me by the collar and kept saying the same thing as he said before. I was so terrified I couldn't even scream, but there was no one around anyway. He pulled me along a path toward Delaware Park Lake. Then he said, "Come on, let's run for a while," still holding the knife where I could see it, about a foot away from my face and hanging onto my coat front. We ran and walked for about 150 to 200 yards and finally he pushed me off the path into a cubby hole of bushes.

Then he ordered me to take my pants down and I took them down, but not my panties. He got really angry and said, "All the way down!" and pushed me down to the ground. He untied the string of his jogging suit pants and bent down and flung my legs back and for a while he just held the knife to me, at the vaginal area. I was sure he was going to butcher me with it and I kept screaming, "Please don't hurt me." Then he said, "Okay," and he forced his penis into my vagina. Then after he was through, which was not too long a time, he got up, pulled up his pants and said, "Give me thirty seconds," and he took off.

The woman watched her attacker backtrack along the route they had come. She quickly dressed and dashed toward the Scajaquada Expressway, crossing when there was a break in traffic. After returning home, she called a gynecologist, who advised her to undergo a rape kit at Erie County Medical Center. The hospital contacted police.

The next page captured Patronik's attention.

"I came upon a one-page police report from 1981," he said. "I have no idea how it even wound up there. Somebody probably didn't know where exactly to put it, so slid it into that folder two decades ago."

It was a General Offense Report, familiar in cop jargon as "an 1191." The photocopied page cited a bizarre encounter by the rape victim. Three days after the incident, she had left her house for the first time since the attack, traveling to the Boulevard Mall in Amherst with her sister.

She scanned the crowd while walking the concourse. Questions and self-doubt seemed more tangible here. Being raped is a life-changing experience. Would the world ever appear as it had just days earlier? Moreover, might strangers glance at her face and see trauma forever etched behind her eyes?

Suddenly she tensed, reaching for her sister's arm. Nearby, a stocky olive-skinned man walked alongside a blonde woman, pushing an infant's stroller. Her mind raced. Disbelief was staggering. *That's him*, she knew. *That's the man who raped me.* Their eyes met, and he turned apprehensive as well. Quickly, he hustled the woman and baby away.

She dashed to a pay phone and contacted Amherst police, while her sister trailed the man. He exited the mall toward the parking lot, getting into a blue Oldsmobile before driving away. The license plate was recorded as he disappeared.

"The statement said the victim was positive this was her attacker," Patronik recounted. "I was skeptical because the rape was so fresh in her head, and obviously she wanted the bad guy caught. Maybe she had identified a suspect just to put her mind at ease. But because she was so insistent, I had to give it some credence."

The rape had occurred outside their jurisdiction, so Amherst authorities turned over the complaint to Buffalo police. Ownership of the car was traced to a Prospect Avenue man named Wilfredo Caraballo.

In 1981, detectives visited his home to conduct an interview. The twenty-eight-year-old Caraballo said that his vehicle had no insurance, had not been on the road for months, and that the complainant must be mistaken. Police read Caraballo his rights, but he had an alibi during the time of the rape. He had no police record. His wife had black hair, so she was not likely to be the woman spotted with the suspect at the mall. Still, detectives asked if they could take his picture, and he agreed. Three shots were snapped while Caraballo sat in his living room. Police would not bother him again, he was assured, once it was proven he had no involvement in the Delaware Park rape.

His photo was put into an array and shown to the rape victim, who could not identify her attacker.

The lead hit a dead end. That was all the old file revealed.

Sitting at his desk, Patronik turned introspective. He phoned Savage for a second opinion.

"There might be something to this," he offered, seconding Patronik's suspicion.

Perhaps the victim had seen her attacker and written the correct license number, but simply failed to make the proper identification. Could Caraballo be the rapist they were searching for?

Patronik tried to run Caraballo's crime history through the computer, but encountered an obstacle. Although he had used the system earlier that day, his three-year certification had expired at an inopportune time. He could complete an online test to become re-certified, but that process took a few hours. Patronik glanced at the clock. It was nearing 8:00 p.m., too late to begin. He was alone in the office, so there was no one else who could log onto the system. It was time to go home.

Before leaving for the night, he called Rozansky and asked the detective to meet him at the command center Saturday morning. They would use Rozansky's ID for computer access.

"Saturday morning I was out with my granddaughter having breakfast," Delano recalled. "We stopped into Oak Street so I could show her the office. Alan and Scott were reading files. They opened the folder from 1981. I immediately thought, *Holy shit, this looks promising.* Our thinking was we needed to get ahold of the victim and the car's owner, Caraballo. Let's have her look at his picture again."

Using state records, Rozansky was able to access Caraballo's driver's license photo. Detectives were intrigued to see that he matched a description of the Bike Path Rapist.

"He was Hispanic with a receding hairline," Delano noted. "We thought maybe he was our guy. That's when the team went looking for him."

In the process, the case broke wide open.

While task force members honed in on Caraballo, Josh Keats worked a different angle, tracking the ten men from his list of Hispanics arrested for solicitation.

"I began visiting each of the suspects, asking for a DNA swab," Keats recalled. "On Monday, January 8, I started my week by going to a house in Cheektowaga. The guy's name was Altemio Sanchez. I planned to say, *Hi, I'm with the state police. I know you were interviewed in Amherst many years ago, but DNA technology has come far. No one will ever bother you again if you can just give us a DNA swab so we can eliminate you as a suspect.* I knocked on Sanchez's door, but no one was home."[14]

Meanwhile, detectives hoping to speak with Caraballo learned he no longer lived in Western New York. He had moved to North Carolina several years earlier. Consulting databases, crime analyst Betsy Schneider cobbled together a family tree on Caraballo. It appeared several relatives still lived locally.

"We planned to pick off Caraballo's family one by one," Rozansky said. "The goal was to get DNA from them to see if the Bike Path Rapist was related. We wanted to know if we were heading in the right direction."

Charting a family tree is not an exact science. Information in the public domain may be limited. Misspellings or similar names can lead to confusion. Often, old-fashioned police work is needed to confirm identities.

---

[14] Keats speculated how the case might have unfolded differently had Sanchez been home. Would advance warning have allowed a killer to escape?

"I don't think so," Keats reflected later. "He had too much of an investment in community to flee. He had beaten cops before, so he would probably think he could do it again. At the same time, I don't see why he would have given me his DNA. I would have been forced to get it a different way, like follow him around until he dropped a cigarette."

"Sometimes you just have to run the leads down to find who you're looking for," Savage explained. "When we were investigating Wilfredo, we came up with the name Margarita Torres. We didn't know for sure, but thought she was his sister. No one answered when we knocked on the door of her house, but one of the neighbors told us she's a cleaner at D'Youville College."

Savage and Rozansky traveled to the college on Buffalo's west side and spoke to a supervisor, who brought Torres before the investigators. Cooperation was not forthcoming.

"She wasn't 100 percent honest with us," Savage recalled. "We showed her Wilfredo's picture and she goes, *Well, this kind of looks like him, but I'm not sure.* I mean, it's her brother. She was covering. She didn't know why we were there and wondered if he was in trouble. She couldn't tell us where he lived. Well, she knew."

"It got me thinking that maybe Caraballo was the Bike Path Rapist, and she wanted to point us in the wrong direction," Rozansky said. "Maybe she knew all this time."

Detectives asked if there was another sibling named Heriberto Sanchez Caraballo, whose name had surfaced in a search for relatives. Torres provided a Fargo Avenue address, but said no one in her family used the surname Sanchez. A quick trip to that house found nobody home.

"He wasn't there, but the name Sanchez was printed on the mailbox," Savage noted sourly.

The family tree raised an unusual connection. Caraballo was an uncle of Altemio Sanchez, the name Keats had pursued the day before. Sanchez's mother, now deceased, was a sister to Wilfredo Caraballo, Margarita Torres, and Heriberto Sanchez Caraballo.

"This was not huge," Patronik admitted, "but it was interesting."

Keats and Rozansky agreed to keep tabs on family connections and mention them when relatives were interviewed.

On January 10, Patronik and Rozansky found Heriberto Sanchez Caraballo at his home. Although he struggled to understand English, his girlfriend translated. Heriberto agreed to submit a DNA sample. But instead of scraping his cheek, he inserted a buccal swab down his throat, and began to gag. Detectives helped him through the process correctly.

"I told him he was not our target, but the DNA would allow us to figure out if we were on the right track," Rozansky said. "I wanted to see if the numbers were close."

The DNA sample was sealed in a plastic bag. On their way out, Rozansky left a business card with his cell phone number scrawled across the top. "If you have contact with Wilfredo in North Carolina," he said, "tell him to give me a call."

Patronik and Rozansky planned to lay out a map pinpointing where each of the Bike Path Rapist's attacks had occurred. Because they were nearby, they ventured to a rape site near Military Road and Hertel Avenue to take a GPS reading.

"We were in the car at a junkyard and Al's phone rang," Patronik recalled. "It was Wilfredo from North Carolina. We figure the brother called Wilfredo just after we left and gave him the number. I was in the driver's seat, so Al put the phone on speaker so we could both listen."

"Detective, I understand you're looking for me," Caraballo said, his voice thick with a Spanish accent.

Before Rozansky had a chance to ask questions about the bike path or long-ago rapes, Caraballo said, "Is this about that thing twenty-five years ago?"

Both detectives paused for a beat, looking at each other with raised eyebrows.

"You tell me," Rozansky replied.

Caraballo sighed. "I wasn't completely honest back then. My nephew Altemio was driving the car that day."

"Who was? What's the name?"

"Altemio. Altemio Sanchez."

Closing the Net

The name sounded familiar to Rozansky, but he could not place it. A few seconds passed before recognition dawned: Altemio Sanchez . . . the suspect Keats was tracking simultaneously.

"I think this is Josh's guy," Rozansky whispered to Patronik, his heart bounding with excitement.

"Altemio was driving your car at that mall?" Rozansky said into the phone.

"Yes, he drive my car," Caraballo answered in halting English.

"Did you ever tell the police?"

Caraballo hesitated. "I don't remember."

Patronik and Rozansky each felt as if fog was evaporating. They sensed that a key piece of the puzzle had just been revealed.

The chat continued for another three minutes, with Caraballo providing contact information and Rozansky promising they would be in touch soon. After he pushed a button to disconnect, Rozansky waved the phone like a wand. "We just found the Bike Path Rapist," he beamed. "Sanchez is our guy!"

Although this was far from proven, Patronik felt an adrenaline rush as well. Vital information had been unearthed after remaining buried for more than a quarter century. There was a reason the rape victim could not identify Caraballo's photo in 1981—he hadn't been driving the car. If the woman was shown a picture of Altemio Sanchez, maybe the case would have proceeded differently.

Both detectives were excited, but Patronik's even temper was not about to succumb to emotion. He quickly phoned Keats, requesting that he relax the quest for Sanchez's DNA. The worst thing that could happen now would be to knock on Sanchez's door and tip him off to the fact he was a suspect.

Sanchez's own vehicle had broken down, so on April 17, 1981, he asked Caraballo's permission to borrow the blue Oldsmobile. Although the car was uninsured, Caraballo loaned Sanchez its keys.

A mere four-year age difference between Caraballo and Sanchez allowed for a nontraditional relationship—more like cousins than uncle and nephew. Growing up on Buffalo's west side, they often played basketball together. Sanchez called his uncle "Freddie." Caraballo referred to Al as "Junior," believing him to be a nice guy.

But Caraballo was unhappy after authorities knocked on his door in 1981. He posed for photos in his living room, knowing they would be shown to a rape victim for identification. Caraballo was not involved in any attacks, so he had little to fear. But after enduring the stigma of a police visit, he wondered if his nephew harbored a secret.

He did not inform detectives that Sanchez borrowed the car, perhaps because he did not want to disclose his role in allowing an unregistered vehicle on the road. Twenty-six years later, he provided a more detailed explanation about why he failed to mention his nephew's name.

Caraballo admitted lying because he was scared. It was intimidating to have authorities show up at his home, so he immediately became reserved. At first he discounted the allegations, not believing Altemio capable of rape. He had heard stories of innocent people who were wrongly jailed, and Caraballo didn't want that to happen to a relative. So he was not forthcoming to police inquiries, but planned to confront Altemio himself. He might discern the truth by gazing into his nephew's eyes.

When the story broke in the media six days after the phone call to Rozansky, Caraballo mentioned all these factors. Of course he had no knowledge that Sanchez was a rapist, he said. Had he been aware, he would have contacted authorities, explaining that by 2007 he had daughters and grandchildren of his own and would not want such a predator loose, relative or not.

Twenty-six years of accumulated silence, however, left reporters asking uncomfortable questions. In that time, a score of attacks had occurred—possibly more unreported—and three women were dead. If Caraballo had told the entire truth in 1981, could all of this have been avoided?

After initially consenting to phone interviews from North Carolina, Caraballo stopped talking as revelations became more damning. One of the last things he told a columnist was that his conscience was clean.

Before his self-imposed silence, however, he admitted confronting his nephew in 1981. Caraballo asked Sanchez if he had done something wrong. Sanchez denied it, but Caraballo didn't entirely believe his nephew. Darkness lurked within those eyes. Sanchez was lying.[15]

That instinct was the reason Caraballo finally confessed the truth, however belatedly.

After speaking with Caraballo in the early afternoon, Patronik called a meeting on Oak Street at 3:00 p.m., where the team began investigating Sanchez in earnest. As information accumulated, he vaulted to the forefront of the suspect pool. Excitement was tangible.

"All the dominoes began to fall quickly," Patronik recalled. "We had a good description from 1992 that the person who solicited Majane Mazur was driving a white Pontiac four-door Sunbird. We checked records and Sanchez owned that car back in 1992. We went to

---

[15] After Sanchez was sentenced in August 2007, he told an Assistant District Attorney that he confessed to his uncle in 1981 that he committed a rape. In that same interview, however, Sanchez lied about facts and contradicted himself when confronted with evidence.

"I believe Sanchez was trying to get back at Wilfredo because that's why he was caught," Delano mused. "Sanchez was angry so he made that story up. On the other hand, Wilfredo knew Sanchez did something wrong while he had the car. Otherwise, why would police come to his house?"

Some members of the task force believe Caraballo knew the truth and kept quiet for twenty-six years. It is more likely, however, that after his arrest Sanchez tried to implicate his uncle as "revenge" for informing investigators about him in the first place.

Sanchez's workplace and pulled personnel files. All the attacks occurred during times he was off shift. In fact, the payroll people had made a notation that he snuck out early one day and it was on the day of a rape. Maybe he thought he would be listed at work and could use that as an alibi if he were ever questioned. With all this information lining up, everyone on the task force was cranked."

Optimism, however, needed to be tempered. There had been other promising suspects before, but those had flamed out. Facts would carry this investigation, not raw emotion.

"Everyone was excited," Keats confirmed, "but Nigrelli and Patronik were good at talking people down from ledges. We were working ourselves into a frenzy. Still, when we started examining Sanchez, I'll be damned if we couldn't make a good circumstantial case against him. He was physically at two of the scenes, identified by a co-worker from American Brass. The last time Majane Mazur's boyfriend saw her, she was getting into the same type of car Sanchez owned. He had been arrested one block away from the Huron Hotel where Mazur lived."

Couple that promising circumstantial evidence with Sanchez's physical appearance, which matched witness descriptions, and the task force became convinced they had their man—but DNA would make or break the case.

Dr. Simich of CPS contacted the task force office with lab results of the buccal swab from Heriberto Sanchez Caraballo. Heriberto was not the Bike Path Rapist, but no one had expected him to be. Nor was the DNA close enough to be the rapist's brother, which eliminated

Wilfredo as well. But the investigators were getting warm. According to Simich, markers indicated a familial link between the examined sample and the killer. Statistically, there is a familiar relationship usually found in first cousins.

Simich had no idea that their most promising suspect was related to Heriberto. Did they have to be cousins?

"He couldn't say definitively," Patronik said. "Everything with him is about statistics. But an uncle-nephew relationship would be consistent with evidence."

Sanchez was looking even better.

Who Was Sanchez?

Authorities had first been alerted to Sanchez in 1990 by a co-worker who spotted him on the Ellicott Creek Bike Path. He had visited the Amherst police station for a voluntary interview and even submitted fingerprint samples before being released. But his Hispanic surname and two subsequent arrests for patronizing prostitutes linked him to the FBI profile. Now the task force had him in their sights. They studied fifteen-year-old paperwork and checked law enforcement reports.

Al Sanchez was born in Puerto Rico on January 19, 1958, the son of Lucy Caraballo and Altemio Sanchez. He had an older brother and two sisters. In the early 1960s, young Al moved to Florida with his mother amid allegations of marital troubles between his parents. His father later resided in New Jersey, but was never a part of Al Jr.'s life.

After living near Miami, how and when Lucy Caraballo arrived in Western New York is unclear, but she initially moved to North Collins, a rural community south of Buffalo. New York State issued Al a Social Security number in the early 1970s and the fatherless family relocated to the city. As a youth, Al attended Buffalo's School No. 1 and then Grover Cleveland High School, graduating in 1977.

While studying at Buffalo State College in 1978, he met his future wife, Kathleen, and they began dating. Sanchez kept an apartment on Parkdale Avenue, not far from campus, adjacent to Delaware Park. On July 5, 1980, the couple married and moved to West Ferry Street. Their son, Christopher, was born in October. Less than a year later, in September 1981, they welcomed a second boy, Michael.

Sanchez never finished college, working at Trico, a local factory, before taking a job at American Brass in 1983.[16] Around that time, he and Kathleen lived on Inwood Place in Buffalo, but in 1986, they purchased a home on Allendale Drive in neighboring Cheektowaga and remained there for more than twenty years.

Active in sports, Sanchez was a jogger, a youth baseball coach, and avid golfer. He worked out regularly at an Amherst health club.

In May 1991, while driving a white 1988 Pontiac Sunbird, he was arrested on Virginia Street in Buffalo for solicitation. In September 1999, he was again caught with a prostitute, this time on Congress Street. Both

---

[16] The company's name changed several times over the years. By 2007, American Brass was called Luvata.

charges were reduced to loitering, and Sanchez paid a fine.

Once Kathleen became aware of the first arrest, domestic tension was tangible. Sometime between 1993 and 1994, after Altemio's vasectomy, he moved out of their Cheektowaga home because his wife believed he was having an affair. Within several weeks, the couple reconciled.

While examining this seemingly average life, members of the task force speculated. Far from ordinary, was Sanchez leading a double existence as a rapist and killer?

As he leapfrogged to become the primary suspect, authorities quietly began trailing Sanchez without his knowledge.

"By the second week in January, we started round-the-clock surveillance on him," Patronik said. "We followed him from work to his house. Four different cars were used so he wouldn't be aware of us, and we posted a vehicle at either end of his street so he couldn't leave without us knowing about it."

While Sanchez appeared promising, a few insiders believed the surveillance was a waste of time. Amherst police had cleared him after their interview fifteen years earlier. Why should he be investigated again?

"Some members said our task force was working in the wrong direction," Rozansky recalled. "Instead of going backwards, we should be looking at tips filing in.

Amherst was disseminating those tips. They thought the answer would be uncovered there, but it wasn't. The solution lurked in the old cases."

Because of his arrests for solicitation, Sanchez's pistol permit had been suspended. But he had never turned in the weapon, as the law required. Two sheriff's detectives visited his Cheektowaga home to collect the gun. Their secondary assignment was to examine Sanchez and secretly secure a DNA sample.

"His gun was an automatic," Patronik said. "To load and unload it, you need to pull back the top. Normally, you don't want a suspect anywhere near a weapon, but our guys had him rack it several times, hoping to get DNA if any skin remnants stuck to the metal."

Sanchez was offered a pen. After signing a receipt for the gun, the officer slid the pen into his pocket. Once back in the car, he bagged the pen in plastic, knowing it could be processed for DNA as well.

Neither ruse worked, however. Within a day, results came back as inconclusive.

"People mistakenly think the last person to touch something leaves DNA, but that's not always the case," Patronik explained. "There was no DNA on the gun, and the pen came back with DNA that was not a match. It was probably our officer's DNA sample."

After a week in which so much progress had been made, the task force was still not able to prove Sanchez was the Bike Path Rapist. By Friday, January 12—seven days after Patronik first discovered the police report that began this investigative path—morale dipped again.

"We left that night with our heads down," Patronik recalled. "We were living this thing. I told myself, if this guy's not the Bike Path Rapist, I'm getting off the task force. We were so close, but couldn't secure a DNA match."

Once home, Patronik did not stop thinking about the case. His mind ruminated, even while trying to focus on other things. With his family tucked away in bed, he paced the floor, finally phoning Rozansky.

"I can't sleep," he lamented.

"I'm wide awake too," Rozansky replied.

Proof

Several attempts to secure DNA from Sanchez had failed. Rather than allow frustration to overtake them, members of the task force gathered to plot their next move. Circumstantial evidence lined up, but scientific confirmation was needed. A DNA sample would prove conclusively whether Altemio Sanchez was the Bike Path Rapist.

Keats could continue to pursue Sanchez for a voluntary DNA swab. But that would alert Sanchez that he was firmly on the radar, especially on the heels of having his gun confiscated.

"If we had gone to Sanchez and asked for his DNA, he would have known we think it's him," Rozansky reflected. "Then he could either flee or kill himself or think, hey, I'm going to get in one more rape or killing. That would not have been the appropriate way to get DNA even if we had a court order."

Delano offered his experience as a homicide investigator. He knew there were ways to secure DNA without the suspect's knowledge. In police lingo, an "abandoned sample" is an item that contains DNA left in a public place. Delano recommended finding an abandoned sample, testing it for proof, then using that data to secure an arrest warrant. As a cold case investigator, he had employed the method before.

"For this to stand up in court, there has to be no expectation of privacy," Delano explained. "If you throw a cigarette on the street, anyone can get it. That's a legitimate sample. If a cop sneaks onto your porch and grabs silverware after you've had a cookout, that's not legal."

Patronik was unsure about the abandoned sample tactic and hesitated. The procedure needed to be perfect, because when the case came to trial, he did not want a judge to dismiss on a technicality. While its merits were undergoing debate, Delano's frustration boiled over.

"It's the only time I was ever mad at Scott," Delano confessed. "I told him he was going to blow this case because of his inexperience."

Patronik sought legal advice from Ken Case, an Erie County assistant district attorney. Case, a veteran lawyer affiliated with the homicide bureau for seven years, had been involved with this investigation since the early days of Joan Diver's disappearance.

In his mid-forties, Case has a smooth voice and resembles an older version of Ron Howard's Richie Cunningham character from *Happy Days*. Task force members respected his skill and honesty.

"I was there for legal questions," he said. "They would sit me down and say, here's what we have. Where do we go from here?"

There was a promising suspect, the ADA was told, but the task force would not reveal his name. That way

Case could not inform his boss, Frank Clark, if ordered to share information.

"They brought me into the conference room and it was like being back in a classroom," Case recalled. "To their credit, they wouldn't give me the suspect's name because they didn't want to put me in a position where I had to tell Frank Clark. Up to this point, many felt he had compromised the investigation. The minute my foot crossed the threshold to his office, he was on the phone with channels 2, 4, and 7. He had even told the media we didn't have DNA on Joan Diver's body. That's not the kind of information you want out there."

What was the best way to secure DNA? Without knowing the argument that had just occurred, Case recommended finding an abandoned sample and having it tested. It turned out that Delano's method was the best practice.

"I realized Dennis had been right an hour ago," Patronik said. "He's a veteran cop who knew more about that situation than the rest of us."

Case's first suggestion, however, involved a hazy legal area.

"I wanted to follow him to work, see where he parked his car, then swab his door handle," Case admitted. "Believe it or not, the legality of that was borderline. It might have violated his privacy, and we needed to get this one right."

The plan was amended. Detectives would follow Sanchez, hoping he visited a public area where a DNA sample could easily be found.

While the investigation narrowed toward Sanchez, Delano continued to work on behalf of Anthony Capozzi.

He informed an assistant district attorney of his certainty that the wrong man had been convicted.

"I showed Ken Case the chart and told him Capozzi was innocent," Delano said. "He didn't want to deal with it right away because we needed to catch the rapist first. I assume he went and informed his boss."

The task force had yet to engage directly with district attorney Frank Clark. Animosity had been brewing between the two sides, and it was about to snowball.

In the late afternoon on Saturday, January 13, Rozansky and Amherst detective Ed Monan parked at the end of Allendale Road. On the neighborhood's opposite side, Keats and Chris Weber of the state police idled in another unmarked car. Sanchez was home, and the four-some maintained surveillance on him. When Keats and Weber broke off for the night, Rozansky and Monan remained on vigil, occasionally relocating from one end of the street to the other.

The home, number 76, is a modest two-story covered in white vinyl siding and pastel blue shutters. A bow window protrudes toward a flowerbed adjacent to the front door's gable. Before the single-car garage, a metal post anchors a basketball hoop. The yard and its surrounding properties are tidy and well maintained. One block east is St. Aloysius Gonzaga Catholic Church, where the Sanchezes were parishioners. Eggert Road, one street to the west, is the dividing line between Cheektowaga and the city of Buffalo.

As detectives passed by the house, Sanchez pulled out of the driveway and drove toward them. Unobtrusively, they reversed direction and shadowed as Sanchez traveled toward Main Street and turned right, heading into Clarence.

"He's a slow driver, and it's hard to follow someone who goes slowly because you become conspicuous," Monan noted. "Sanchez and his wife pulled to the side of the road, like they were looking at a map. They may have been checking for a restaurant's address, and realized they went too far. They turned around and came back down Main."

Sanchez pulled into the parking lot of the Walker Plaza in Amherst before entering Sole Restaurant. Rozansky and Monan waited a few minutes, then proceeded after them, standing at the bar while the couple dined at a nearby table. Neither officer had ever interviewed Sanchez, so there was little chance he realized he was under observation.

It was a Saturday night, and the dining room was busy. Detectives were intrigued to see Sanchez up close. Muscular and stocky, he was bald on top, with salt-and-pepper hair cropped close above his ears. He wore a mustache and goatee flecked with gray. His eyes were dark marbles. Likewise, it was the first time they had glimpsed his wife, Kathleen. In her late forties, she had a rounded face with dark hair.

"I got in touch with the restaurant manager and asked the server not to clear their table," Monan recalled. "The couple was within our view the entire time."

Officers were told it would reflect badly on management if dishes and cutlery were allowed to accumulate in front of customers. They agreed, however, to leave some remnants untouched after the couple had eaten.

Savage and fellow sheriff Greg McCarthy joined the stakeout, waiting in the parking lot with plastic evidence bags. When the Sanchezes pushed away their chairs and stood, Savage and McCarthy started the car, prepared to continue the tail. Monan and Rozansky slid on latex gloves.

"We collected a dish, a straw, and a linen napkin, which turned out to be a real find," Monan said. "The silverware had already been cleared, which bothered me. I would have liked a spoon or fork, something he put into his mouth."

Evidence was taken back to the Amherst police station, where it was repackaged and transported to the CPS lab.

"Until it was put in the car, I never let it out of my sight," Monan recalled. "I knew this would be crucial if I had to testify."

The second team followed the Sanchezes to Borders bookstore on Walden Avenue in Cheektowaga, across from the Galleria Mall. Savage and McCarthy waited inconspicuously while the couple sat in the tiled cafe drinking coffee. The mug he used was confiscated after Sanchez walked away.

"The plan was to get as many samples as we could," Rozansky explained. "Suppose our attempt at Sole had failed?"

With potentially new DNA evidence, CPS lab was on standby.

"I called Dr. Simich and asked if he could do another DNA test," Patronik said. "He was not crazy about the idea because it was the weekend, but he changed plans to go skiing with his family on Sunday and came in to work. He told me we would have results in sixteen hours."

After Savage and McCarthy took Sanchez's coffee cup downtown to the CPS lab, they drove to the Amherst police station to retrieve Savage's truck. Savage wanted to make another pass by Sanchez's house, where two new teams were conducting surveillance to be sure the suspect did not flee.

A sheriff's tandem was parked to the left of Sanchez's house, out of sight around a curve. While they could not see the home, they would be aware if Sanchez exited the neighborhood in that direction.

Two officers from Amherst covered the other route. At the curb, three doors away, they kept the engine running and the heater on.

Savage cruised along the street, waved to his fellow officers, and did a double take. Sanchez's Ford Windstar was not in the driveway.

Maybe I missed it, he thought. *Maybe he parked it on the road.*

Savage looped around and made another pass. Kathleen's car, which had been driven to Sole and Borders earlier that evening, was in the driveway. But the minivan was nowhere to be seen.

"Where's Sanchez?" Savage asked, rounding the curve and wedging his truck parallel to the sheriffs on watch.

"At the house."

"I didn't see his van. I drove by a couple times."

The deputies were bewildered. "It was there when we got here," they said. "It didn't pass by us."

Savage drove down the street to the Amherst officers on duty.

"Where's Sanchez?" he repeated.

Again, the answer came. "He's in the house."

"So where's his van?" Savage wondered.

The cop behind the wheel scratched his head. "I don't know. We're watching the car."

As the officer realized that their subject had eluded them, blood drained from his face. Savage was furious and incredulous.

"They didn't see him come out of the house, get in his van, and pass by them," he fumed. "When I realized what happened, I had to think Sanchez made us. It was a cold January night and you could see exhaust coming out of their tailpipe. He would have to be blind to drive by two guys sitting in an Impala with the engine running and not know they were cops."[17]

On Savage's orders, the sheriff's car raced from the neighborhood toward Luvata, formerly American Brass, where Sanchez worked. His Windstar was in the parking lot. It appeared the surveillance team had not been spotted after all.

---

[17] Savage said the next time he saw those two officers was four months later, when a *Buffalo News* photographer appeared to take a group photo of men and women who contributed to solving the case. "They showed up to get their picture taken," he said with disdain. "Everybody wants to wet their beak in the glory. If I was them, I'd be ashamed. I wouldn't want my name anywhere near this thing after I'd blown an assignment like that."

"You've Got Him"

As members of the task force gathered at Oak Street on
Sunday, everyone kept one eye on the clock. An aura of
electricity permeated the air. Whenever a phone chirped,
it was quickly answered. To combat anticipation, those
who had tailed Sanchez the night before reflected on their
first-hand observations of him. Older now, he appeared
softer and less hostile than in the 1991 mug shots taken
after his solicitation arrest.

Discussions evolved from Sanchez to his wife.
Everyone had concerns about Kathleen. Did the rape
victim at Boulevard Mall spot her with Sanchez in 1981?
Could she have been blonde twenty-five years ago? Now,
her face and body had been widened by time, and her
shoulder-length hair was dark. Had it been bleached or
dyed over the years? More intriguing, perhaps, was this:
If her husband was the Bike Path Rapist, how much did
she know about his crimes?

A ringing phone interrupted the banter. It was not
the lab's anticipated call.

"We were as anxious as a new father waiting in the
delivery room," Rozansky recalled.

After hours of pacing, the team gathered in the conference room to share pizza for dinner. With them was
ADA Ken Case. Patronik's cell phone rang. He answered,
spoke briefly with Simich, then pressed the speaker
function and held the phone at arm's length for all to
hear.

Simich said simply, "You've got him."

"We all jumped out of our seats," Case recalled.
"There was hugging and high-fives all around."

"When we got the call that DNA matched, I was screaming," Rozansky recalled. "I was dancing, yelling, 'We got this guy! We finally got him!'"

The focus shifted from investigation into arrest mode. Sanchez was in the warehouse that Sunday night. The plan was choreographed with input from the district attorney's office: Officers would tail him leaving the factory when his shift ended, then initiate a curbside stop and make an arrest near his home. Savage, Rozansky, Monan, and McCarthy—the same team that followed Sanchez Saturday night—were selected for the job.

"We wanted to get him out of his environment," Patronik explained. "Let him drive toward Cheektowaga, then we would pull him over and search the car. We didn't want him to get to his house."

Case spent the evening hours preparing a search warrant for the Sanchez residence.

Monday, January 15, dawned gray and rainy. Because it was Martin Luther King Day and schools were not in session, there was less traffic than normal. As Sanchez left work before daybreak, two unmarked cars lagged behind.

"The weather was lousy, with wet sleet," Savage said. "Sanchez started driving all over the place. It's hard to follow somebody without them knowing it, especially if there's not much traffic. I worried again that he had made us and we were going to get burned."

Sanchez traveled to a doctor's office on Millersport Highway in Amherst. Watching him enter the building gave Savage an uneasy feeling. He requested additional cars to join the pursuit so Sanchez could not evade them.

"The whole time we were thinking the guy must know something's going on," Savage noted. "Is he going to make a break for it? Is he going to go in the front door and duck out the back? It was a big building and we didn't have enough people to cover every exit."

While they watched, Sanchez emerged from the office and reentered his van. Using highways 290 and 190, he circled closer to downtown and Buffalo's west side. Cruising along Niagara Street, Savage believed it was time for action.

"I got on the phone with the command post," Savage said. "I told them we had to make a decision here. He was only driving a minivan, but we still didn't want to get into a chase with this guy. Does he have a gun? Is he going to go someplace and take a hostage? What's going to happen? It was clear he wasn't going home. We could be doing loops around the city all day long."

Patronik agreed. "When Sanchez's driving became erratic, I gave the order to take him immediately, even though it was before we originally intended."

While Savage and Patronik spoke, Sanchez turned onto Gelston Street, along Buffalo's west side. Near a warehouse, Sanchez stopped along the left curb after recognizing he was being followed. One unmarked car nosed in behind him, and another quickly blocked the front to prevent escape. Savage emerged from his car and approached the van.

"What's going on?" Sanchez asked, voice drizzled with a Puerto Rican accent.

"We need to talk to you," Savage answered, heightened senses ready for the slightest movement, for anything out of the ordinary. But Sanchez was serene and even-tempered. Standing this close, Savage recognized Sanchez's stocky frame and thick neck.

"He was very calm," Savage recalled. "We got him out of the vehicle and searched him thoroughly. There was no intent to question him until he was back at the office. We didn't read him his rights at that point because he wasn't under arrest. He was handcuffed, put in our car, and taken to West Eagle Street."

Sheriff's headquarters was only blocks away, so the decision was made to transport him there. A tow truck impounded the minivan, and it was stored until a search warrant was secured.

There were no apparent jitters from the serial killer who had eluded capture for so long.

"For a guy who had done everything he had, Sanchez was remarkably composed," Savage reflected. "His attacks happened as far back as the 1970s—almost thirty years. He must have decided long ago that if the cops ever get him, he's not going to break down and confess. He's going to deny, stay cool, and not get worked up. That's exactly how he played it."

Women

Buffalo detective Lissa Redmond does not look like a cop. She more resembles an actress from *CSI* or *NYPD Blue*. In her mid-thirties, she is petite with shoulder-length brown hair and bright eyes, a far cry from the stereotype of a brash city detective.

"No one looks at me and thinks I'm a cop," she said, "but once I started the police academy, I knew it was for me."

Although Redmond originally planned to become a lawyer, she scored well on the police exam, and her career took off. She was promoted to detective at age twenty-seven, and discovered her niche in the Sex Offense Squad. This was where she first encountered the Bike Path Rapist files, examining his last known attack in 1994.

"My lieutenant plopped a booklet in front of me that was assembled by Amherst police," Redmond recalled. "It had details about the unsolved rapes and Linda Yalem's murder. There was one remaining rape where the statute of limitations had not run out. Tips filtered in from *Unsolved Mysteries*. My partner and I located boxes of evidence and files from old cases.

"Although we never stopped investigating, the biggest problem was that interest had waned because several years went by without any activity. It was out of the public's eye, so it became a side project we worked on when our regular caseload slowed down."

Redmond took a three-month leave from the job on October 1, 2007, two days after the Diver homicide. Although she was away from work, Delano was in frequent contact for her knowledge of long-ago rapes. On January 1, when her leave ended, she reported to Oak Street. She was the last person to join the task force, and the entire case broke in the span of five days.

While Sanchez was taken into custody, Redmond participated in a different drama unfolding simultaneously at his Cheektowaga home. Knowing the suspect's wife was inside, Redmond was one of three officers who kept surveillance from across the street.

It was a wet morning as Redmond was on watch with Chris Weber of the state police and Mike Rose of the Amherst police. Kathleen emerged from the house, rushing through the rain to the parked car in the driveway. She was preparing to leave for work when officers displaying badges stepped onto the property to introduce themselves. She wanted to know what this was about and was nervous enough that she asked to see Redmond's ID twice.

"We were reluctant to tell her too much in the driveway," Redmond said. "Because of the rain, we wondered if we could go into the garage. She let us in and we explained that her husband was a suspect in the bike path rapes. She couldn't believe it, and agreed to come to the Amherst police station, where one of her sons met her."

By 2007, the Sanchez boys were twenty-five and twenty-six years old. One son, Michael, remained in Western New York, while the older, Christopher, lived in California.

Inside a quiet room at the station, Redmond explained the evidence to Kathleen Sanchez. She was stunned, refusing to believe her husband capable of such crimes.

One of the most frequently debated questions surrounding the aftermath of Sanchez's arrest involves his wife. How could Kathleen not have known she shared a life with a serial killer? Was Al a masterful liar or was Kathleen exceedingly naïve?

Having interviewed both husband and wife, Redmond has since asked the same questions herself.

"She is a lovely woman who couldn't have been nicer," Redmond said. "Mrs. Sanchez was so convinced of her husband's innocence that she gave us permission to search their house. She even showed us the calendar and pointed out the day we told her Joan Diver was killed. They went to a party that night, and pictures were taken that later surfaced in the *Buffalo News*."

On the evening of September 29, a photo taken in a downtown bar captures the couple in a candid moment. Wearing a white polo shirt with one button open at the neck, the handwritten nametag "Al Sanchez" is pasted on his chest. Kathleen's right arm reaches behind her husband, purse straps visible against her shoulder, while the sticker "Kathy Sanchez" is affixed to her jacket's lapel. Although gazing in different directions, both display open-mouthed smiles.

How could Sanchez have strangled Joan Diver that morning, then laugh at a cocktail party by sunset?

"When I saw that photo, it didn't surprise me," Delano said. "This guy had no sense of remorse whatsoever. His victims were not human beings as far as he was concerned. The thing that puzzles me is how he could love his wife and kids if that's how little he thought of human life."

"Their marriage had its ups and downs, but I really believe Mrs. Sanchez had no idea what her husband was doing," Redmond reflected. "They went on cruises, they went camping, they went bowling, they went to parties together. She thought she was living an average everyday marriage. It was just unfathomable for her that her husband could be the Bike Path Rapist."

While Redmond spoke with Kathleen Sanchez in Amherst, the interrogation of her husband progressed slowly. Thinking Sanchez might respond differently if a woman posed questions, Redmond was requested downtown. Called off from Kathleen's interview, a car with sirens and flashing lights rushed her along the Kensington Expressway to the sheriff's office on West Eagle Street.

After victimizing so many women, Altemio Sanchez was about to have the tables turned on him.

Initial Interview

Dennis Delano is a perfectionist. In his quest to be an outstanding detective, he places a premium on strength of character and smart decision-making.

When fellow public servants stray from standard practices or try to cut corners, Delano objects; he sometimes lashes out in frustration and alienates those around him. Long after the initial interview with Altemio Sanchez occurred at the sheriff's office, Delano still believed it should have unfolded differently.

A plan had been scripted in which Sanchez would be delivered to the command center on Oak Street, where Delano, Keats, and Monan would interrogate him.

"It was pre-determined that certain people should conduct the interview," Delano said. "I was one of them because I have experience with homicides and cold cases. Josh Keats is a homicide investigator, so it made sense that he be part of it too. The sheriff's department doesn't investigate many murders, so they're less experienced with the procedure. Although Amherst police only had a handful of homicides in the last twenty years, Ed Monan was going to be included because of their affiliation with the Yalem killing."

When Sanchez was taken into custody, he was transported to the sheriff's office, adjacent to the Erie County Holding Center.

"Within five minutes of Sanchez being arrested, he was undergoing an interview," Delano said sourly. "Now tried and true, standard procedure is you keep a suspect sitting alone for a half hour or hour before you talk to him. Let him think about what's going on. There are certain techniques you have to use or you're not going to get results. I arrived with Ken Case. When we walked in Ed Monan was interviewing Sanchez. A TV was set up so we could watch, but the conversation wasn't being taped. A woman was sitting there with a legal pad trying to write down everything that was being said." Delano shook his head and scowled. "This shouldn't have happened."

Delano believes certain factions were overanxious. Bragging rights could be claimed by the organization that secured a confession. Amherst police in particular were eager to boast that after nearly thirty years they had slammed the lid shut on the Bike Path Rapist case.

Monan reflected that there was no reason to wait before starting the interview, believing that evidence against Sanchez was overwhelming.

"I wanted to get an explanation of what he was doing all these years," Monan said. "I thought when he was confronted with the facts, he would confess."

In fact, the opposite occurred. Despite being in a closed room for nearly ten hours, Sanchez said little of value and steadfastly refused any involvement with a single rape or murder.

❋

Before a drab-colored wall with closed-circuit TV cameras hanging in the corner, onlookers monitored the interview from the next room.

Rozansky and Monan questioned Sanchez, who sat calmly, remaining composed and tight-lipped. The discussion began at 9:45 a.m. and proceeded slowly, with detectives politely asking if Sanchez wanted something to eat or drink.[18] He agreed to a glass of water. It was placed before him, but Sanchez changed his mind and did not touch it. Clad in long sleeves, he casually nudged the cup away with his elbow.

"When somebody mentioned DNA, he must have thought about it and decided he wasn't putting his mouth on any water glass," Savage observed.

Extending courtesies to a suspected serial killer may seem unreasonable, but these things are part of the procedure with any interrogation.

"We offered him food and drink because when you end up in court on a murder charge, you don't want a defense lawyer accusing you of mistreating a client," Monan said. "I explained to Mr. Sanchez very clearly

---

[18] It is better to treat a suspect cordially, according to Delano.

"If a reasonable person thinks he can't leave, he behaves differently. Smart cops will have a suspect come in on their own accord. If he's in custody, you have to read him his Miranda rights, and you try to delay that as long as you can to get the most information. Once handcuffs come out, the interview takes on a different tone."

Sanchez had been handcuffed on the ride to the Sheriff's Office.

that we had his DNA. I told him where he sat in the restaurant and that I watched him eat dinner on Saturday
night. He wouldn't go for it. It was almost like it had been
rehearsed in his mind. He didn't think we had his DNA,
and if we didn't have his DNA, we couldn't link him. He
had no reaction when we told him he was accused of
murder."

District attorney Frank Clark had previously admitted to the media that there had been no DNA found
on Joan Diver's body. The link to the Bike Path Rapist had been recovered inside her truck. Releasing that
tidbit limited Rozansky's range of inquiries during the
interrogation.

"Frank Clark told the world the body was clean,"
Rozansky said. "Why tell the bad guy anything? How do
I bluff for nine hours?"

Monan and Rozansky took turns asking questions,
trying to narrow the list of excuses the killer might
devise. During the morning, Sanchez remained formal
and composed, admitting nothing.

"I understand you're doing your job, but I can't tell
you no more 'cause I didn't do anything," he insisted.

The detectives pressed on, wondering how Sanchez's
wife was reacting to the news that he was the Bike Path
Rapist.

"She would be very upset by what evidence you said
you have," Sanchez reflected. "It would break her heart."
Then, in a rare verbal slip, he said, "If I told her the truth
about what you had it would break up my marriage."

Monan asked if Sanchez was the type of person who
would admit to wrongdoing.

"I'm not the type of person who would do anything like that," he claimed. "I don't have it in me. I used to hunt, but not anything like that."

The only time Sanchez had ever been in Clarence, he said, was to play golf. He had never been on a bike path there. Nor had he ever been to Frontier High School, where a teenager was raped in 1986. His only connection to Hamburg was that he used to play bar-league baseball at an old military base that is now parkland.

Their tone became more aggressive. "You're the Bike Path Rapist," they told Sanchez. "We know you are."

"That's what you say," he replied smugly. In a sedate tone, he unveiled a subtle threat. "Just so you know, I could call a lawyer anytime I want. Right now I choose not to. If you had anything on me, I'd be in jail by now."

"He was trying to taunt us," Monan noted. "He thought he was in control. We sat there for a long time, and he never even went to the bathroom."

Detectives believe Sanchez was playing a game. He had beaten an interview sixteen years earlier, so thought he could again. Rozansky knew they had the right guy. At first he treaded gingerly, fearing Sanchez would request a lawyer and the interview would cease. But as denials kept piling up, Rozansky called them out.

"So what were you doing on the Amherst bike path?" the detective asked, referencing Sanchez's co-worker who reported him there in 1990.

"I was never on the bike path."

"What about Delaware Park?"

"I've never been to Delaware Park either."

"Your wife says you go there," Rozansky pointed out. "Is your wife lying?"

"No."

Later, Rozansky inquired about Sanchez's vasectomy in the early 1990s.

"I didn't have a vasectomy," he answered.

"But your wife told us you did. Is she lying?"

"No."

Several back and forth discussions ensued. He continuously denied having had one, although his wife had confirmed to authorities that he underwent surgery in 1993. Whether Sanchez thought admitting the procedure might connect him to the crime, or remaining mum was simply a macho thing, he finally relented and admitted it was true.

"I just felt embarrassed talking about the vasectomy," he finally confessed. "I don't tell any of my friends about that."

After three and a half hours, it was clear that little progress was being made. The detectives were called from the room, leaving Sanchez alone.

"I told Rozansky to take a break," Patronik said. "During the interim we set up a radio next to Sanchez. We left it on WBEN and the host was having a field day on the air, mentioning Sanchez's name as breaking news. Once his name was broadcast, you could see his shoulders sag."

With the media announcement, Sanchez's anonymity was gone. Even if he did beat this rap, his reputation had already been tarnished. Family, friends, neighbors, co-workers—everyone who thought highly of him—would now have second thoughts.

Approaching 2:00 p.m., sheriff's deputy Greg Mc-
Carthy entered. A new interrogator might connect with
Sanchez and finally penetrate the stonewalling. Discussion turned to Sanchez's childhood and the reasons for
his parents' divorce.

"I don't think you want to know that story," he said
softly. Born in Puerto Rico, his time there was brief.
"When I was two years old, my mother caught my father
with another woman. Six months after that, she packed
us up and we moved to Florida. I was only two but my
brothers and sister later told me what happened."

He saw his father again briefly, years later. The elder
Sanchez died in May 2006.

Allegations arose that Sanchez had an affair with a
woman named Sharon in the mid-1990s. He denied this,
saying only that he knew her but they were never inti-
mate. His wife, however, had confided to detectives that
her husband had moved out for several months while the
couple struggled to save their marriage.

When asked if he had ever abused nieces or neph-
ews, Sanchez grew defensive.

"No, I'm not that fucking crazy, excuse my
language."

By 3:30 p.m., after nearly six hours of fruitless questions, detectives were losing patience. Tension built for
hours, but no progress was being made. Playing the part
of the bad cop, Monan turned hostile, yelling "fuck you,"
while his partner tried to goad Sanchez into an argument.

Rozansky sketched a grim scenario from September
29: Sanchez lurking along the Clarence bike path, impatient for his next random victim. As he looped a ligature
over Joan Diver and dragged her into the underbrush,

she surprised him by fighting back. The struggle was unexpected, and Sanchez became further enraged.

"You're a coward," Rozansky spat. "She kicked your ass in those bushes, and that's why you killed her. You're nothing but a cockroach." He dropped autopsy photos of Diver onto the table between them, aiming a finger at Sanchez's face. "You did this! I know you did this! The whole world is going to know you did this!"

With emotions erupting, Rozansky was called out of the room. The strong-arm approach was not working.

"Those guys were really aggressive," assistant district attorney Ken Case recalled, having watched the proceedings via closed-circuit TV. "They were coming at him hard, but he stayed calm."

As everyone cooled down, McDonald's hamburgers were laid before Sanchez after 4:00 p.m. He had worked all night, and gotten off shift early that morning. He had not eaten or drank anything since leaving the factory, nor slept since the day before. Although he nodded off during a ten-minute interlude that afternoon, he remained alert and refused food.

Sanchez was confident that he would soon be walking out a free man. He did not believe that authorities had his DNA. Because of his repeated denials, detectives offered to swab him again. *If you are innocent,* they claimed, *this will prove it. But we know you're not innocent.*

Sanchez refused to consent to a DNA swab.

Josh Keats relieved the interviewers at 5:00 p.m. He had observed the day's events on closed-circuit TV, and knew that a new track was needed. While Sanchez listened, Keats changed tactics and framed the discussion differently. By being patient and firm, he established an early rapport.

"I watched Rozansky and Monan's interview and that wasn't working," Keats said. He decided to play on Sanchez's emotions. From earlier conversation, Keats gleaned that Sanchez viewed himself as religious. He was a practicing Catholic, a parishioner at a church one block from his home.

"You believe in God," Keats told him. "So now it's time to ask for forgiveness."

But when pressured to list the Ten Commandments, Sanchez could only name two. Keats realized their killer was not as religious as he claimed, so he changed course again.

"What's done is done," Keats explained. "We've got you. We know you did it, and you're not going to be released. What will happen now is that your family is going to be hounded by the media. The only thing that helps your family is to give us answers. That way we can provide those answers to the press so they will stay away from your wife and kids."

Keats asked if Sanchez had ever raped a woman. His response was mumbled and unclear, unrecorded by the stenographer, but Keats heard it and sat up straighter. Speaking crassly, like he was among men at a bar, Sanchez had joked that the only woman he raped was his wife. He immediately regretted his words and disavowed them, claiming it was an unsuccessful attempt at humor.

After forty-five minutes, Lissa Redmond entered, anxious to ask questions. Until now, Sanchez had dealt exclusively with men. Having Redmond in the room unnerved him.

"I don't know where to begin," she said. Sanchez had no way of knowing she had investigated his last known rape in 1994, but her words implied that this was an interview she had often anticipated. "I've been waiting to talk to you for a long time. I just arrived, so I don't know what everyone else has said. But I talked to your wife and I know you've been telling lies. Your wife and son love you so much but they have a lot of questions and I didn't have answers for them. I'm hoping I can give them answers."

Much like his wife a few hours earlier, Sanchez did not believe she was a cop, accusing her of being a psychologist trying to pass herself off as a policewoman.

"Are you really a detective or something that comes in as a shrink?" he wondered.

Redmond noted the use of the word "something," rather than "someone."

Case had proposed the idea of using Redmond to conduct an interview. As onlookers watched, they were stunned at Sanchez's transformation. His passive demeanor evaporated when she entered the room. To further the effect, Keats stepped out so Redmond was the sole questioner.

"Sending in Lissa was an intentional choice," Case recalled. "To do what Sanchez did, you have to understand he hates women. His attorney later said he's got a devil inside him when it comes to females. Rozansky and Monan were aggressive to him, in his face. In spite of that, Sanchez was calm and collected. The minute Lissa came in the room, he turned hostile towards her before she even opened her mouth. He was all over her, so I knew we hit a chord."

After twenty minutes of discussion, Sanchez was still doubtful that Redmond was a cop. He asked again if she was a detective. He had become belligerent in the face of her questions.

"You just want to stare at me in the eyes," he snarled. "You got your job to do. I'm not stupid."

Drawing on her experience with sex crimes, Redmond tried to express empathy. Rapists, she knew, are masters at disassociation. By separating themselves from their actions, they justify their behavior and find a comfort zone that allows them to exist without being overwhelmed by guilt.

"This is not who you are," Redmond told Sanchez. "There's a switch that goes on. You have a demon inside. I understand you can't stop these urges."

Sanchez deliberated. He paused, waiting for her to continue, listening intently. Observers considered that he was experiencing a change of heart. What was happening within his mind? Would he finally lower the façade and confess?

As time passed, Sanchez still offered no explanation.

"Lissa and I had a rapport with him," Keats said, recalling frustration. "But it was tough to make a true connection. Sanchez is a sociopath with no remorse."

Patronik experienced mixed emotions. With the killer in custody, citizens of Western New York were now safer. But the longer this dragged out, the less likely it appeared a revelation would occur.

"Nothing came of it," Patronik said of the long day. "No admission of guilt. Sanchez was convinced he was walking out. He'd been interviewed by Amherst police before and had walked away, so this was just another interview. He didn't believe we had his DNA."

Although no confession was secured, after nine and a half hours, the decision was made to end the interview.

"Steve Nigrelli asked me how much longer this should go on," Case said. "Sanchez hadn't budged. In fact, he was taunting us."

Case inhaled deeply, considering legal ramifications. Recognizing the magnitude of finally capturing a long-sought serial killer, his stomach tightened as he gave the green light. "Go arrest the son of a bitch," he said gravely.

Nigrelli and Keats entered the interview room, asked Sanchez to stand, and patted him down one last time before securing arms behind his back and snapping cuffs around his wrists.

"His expression changed," Case recalled. "It was the first look of concern I'd seen from him all day."

Outside, reporters lingered around the sheriff's building for stray nuggets of news, or a glimpse at the elusive Bike Path Rapist. A cluster of media assembled in Amherst as well.

"The DA tried to determine which murder to prosecute first because with the suspect in custody, the clock was ticking," Patronik said. "To link all three murders at once would have been bad because the clock would run simultaneously. They agreed to charge for one, then pursue others down the line."

LaCorte, the lieutenant from Amherst, expected to take Sanchez from the sheriff's office back to Amherst's jail that night, because the Yalem homicide was the initial charge. Although that would be accepted protocol, Patronik objected to moving the prisoner. The Erie County Holding Center was a secure location, one building away, while Amherst was several miles up Main Street, the next town over, and did not have a level of security equivalent to the county's lockup.

"It didn't make sense for him to be transferred," Patronik said. "The next morning, Amherst would have arraigned him to the holding center anyway."

He phoned his boss, Sheriff Timothy Howard, who agreed with the assessment. Sanchez would be kept downtown. He was booked and taken next door immediately.

Media had gathered outside the Amherst police station, having been alerted that the Bike Path Rapist would be arriving to spend the night in jail. TV stations were set to film the "perp walk" as Sanchez exited the car and was hustled inside. They waited in vain.[19]

Instead, cameras posted at the sheriff's office recorded Sanchez being moved, capturing the first public images of the long-sought killer.

As filmed through a mesh of cyclone fencing, several deputies flanked the prisoner as he walked down

---

[19] Although this angered some on the task force, Patronik is generous when recalling the events. "Amherst has pride in their department and wanted to showcase the fact that this monster was finally off the street."

an incline. Wearing a black sweat jacket and jeans, Sanchez was manacled by the wrists and ankles, limiting his movement to tentative baby steps. With eyes closed, he muttered to himself, lips moving mechanically as if in silent, whispered prayer.

Shock

Within hours, those who knew Altemio Sanchez expressed disbelief that he was a serial rapist and killer. Neighbors grew misty-eyed at the prospect. He had always been normal, so kind and generous. He hosted parties at his house, played with his boys as they grew up, remaining friends with young people even after they passed into adulthood. At Luvata, the factory where he was employed, feelings were similar. Sanchez was considered an exemplary co-worker, volunteering for charitable events, willing to lend a hand to anyone in need. This was a man who looked out for others.

"I have an uncle who worked at American Brass and knew Sanchez," Lissa Redmond admitted. "His reputation was consistent as an all-around nice guy."

Frank Conway had been employed at Luvata for more than ten years when the news broke. Although they worked different shifts, he knew Sanchez and was shocked to learn of his involvement.[20]

---

[20] Conway's connection to the case was unique. "It's strange, but I worked with Al Sanchez and went through four years of high school with Tony Capozzi. We were pretty good friends. Back when Capozzi was convicted, I just didn't believe it. I knew Tony and it just didn't ring true. He never struck me as that type of person."

"The day that he was arrested, I was working on a machine with a couple other guys," he recalled. "The boss came over and said they caught the Bike Path Rapist. We all said, *Hey, that's terrific*. Then he told us it was Al Sanchez. I swore at him and said 'What are you picking on Al for?' That's how much we didn't believe it."

After being captured, serial killers are often categorized as loners, but Sanchez did not fit that profile. In his job as a forklift operator, Sanchez was reliable and respected for his skills. He was part of a fraternity from Luvata who gathered regularly to play golf, sometimes traveling to distant locales like Toronto or South Carolina to tee off along a new or unfamiliar course.

"Of all the people in the place, you'd never suspect him," Conway said. "Everyone agreed on that. It shocked the hell out of us. The mood at work dipped way down for a long time after that. It was terrible. A good friend of mine had been at Al's house a few weeks earlier for a Christmas party. After the arrest, he walked around saying, 'I can't believe this is true.'"

A media contingent parked outside the Luvata plant compounded the tension in days to follow. When entering and exiting the building, Conway and his fellow workers asked reporters to leave them alone. It seemed everyone vied for an angle on how the serial killer passed himself off as an "ordinary guy."

Around Sanchez's Cheektowaga home, neighbors were aghast to learn of his arrest. As police cars parked along Allendale Road during the rainy Monday, residents huddled on the sidewalk trying to pry information from cops while speculating among themselves.

"I will never forget that day," said Janine Drmacich. "It was the worst day of my life. It was the first time I've ever hyperventilated and not been able to breathe. Did you ever have a nightmare where there is an emergency and you're trying to dial the phone but can't? That was my reality."

Drmacich grew up a few doors away from the Sanchezes. Her parents, Jerry and Nadine Donahue, were friendly with Al and Kathleen for more than twenty years. A group of families had moved into the neighborhood during the 1980s, and their core remained strong, even as years accumulated and children grew. Drmacich played with the Sanchez boys when she was younger and considered their house a safe haven.

"I was a latchkey kid and occasionally I'd forget my keys. Because of Al's work schedule, he was one of the few neighbors at home during the day. Whenever I knocked on his door he was wonderful. He'd let me in to call my parents. He would fix me a snack. There were many times when I was alone with him, but I was never uncomfortable."

"I've always been a trusting person," she noted, "but this really throws you. I started evaluating myself. I thought I was a good judge of character. Now I wonder if you can ever really know someone. My mother has had a hard time with that. She's traumatized, less trusting now."

Passing months did not lessen the initial shock.

"As many times as Al's friends have sat down together, there is nothing in hindsight where we say, *Hey, this makes sense now. Remember that one time . . .* ? Nothing

like that. We have all tried to find an event that was a red
flag, but we can't. It wasn't like he overcompensated and
was a good guy in every situation. He just hit that middle
ground so well. He was like any other dad who was great
with his kids."

After Sanchez's arraignment, members of the task force
were summoned to the Erie County District Attorney's
office on Delaware Avenue. Although they had previously dealt with ADA Ken Case during the investigation,
this was their first meeting with his colorful boss, Frank
Clark, regarding the Bike Path Rapist.[21]

Clark, in his mid-sixties, has ruddy cheeks, a square
face, and white hair. He held frequent press conferences,
and as a result he was a mainstay on local TV newscasts.
Clark had an exaggerated method of speaking. Using an
unnatural cadence, he overemphasized words, lips working double time like a novice stage actor long on enthusiasm but devoid of talent. He donned a pseudo-Boston
accent, reminiscent of the Kennedys, in spite of growing
up in Western New York.

Discussion centered around valid evidence that
could be offered at trial. There was a DNA link with the
Yalem and Mazur homicides, so those could be indicted
immediately. But more work was needed to connect the
killer with Diver, because Sanchez's DNA was not found
on her body, only the steering wheel of her SUV.

---

[21] Clark did not respond to calls seeking an interview for this book.

"Coming out of Clark's office, I pulled aside Frank Sedita," Delano noted. Sedita, a deputy district attorney, initially oversaw the Joan Diver homicide before being replaced by Case. Sedita, however, would prosecute Sanchez at trial.

"This Capozzi thing is not going away," Delano recalled telling Sedita. "I'm not sure if your boss knows, but Frank Clark needs to be told about it."

"I have to focus on Sanchez right now," Sedita replied, in a tone Delano described as "prissy."

"I'm making you aware of this," Delano responded. "If we figured out the wrong man is in jail, somebody from the media is going to connect the dots soon enough."

A week went by, and Delano's impatience brewed. He had already written e-mails to the governor and the parole board. After informing two ADAs about the predicament, the problem was no closer to being rectified.

Simultaneously, reporters dogged task force members for any stray nugget of news. Everyone wanted to know how Sanchez had finally been captured. Delano ignored their requests, keeping quiet until chief of detectives Dennis Richards suggested he indulge them and grant interviews.

"I had been avoiding the media," Delano admitted. "They had been calling but I don't like talking to them. I had too much going on to bother with that. When my boss told me to deal with it, in my own mind I thought I would answer questions for a day or two and be done."

Representatives from three local TV channels and several radio stations crammed into the Oak Street conference room. Delano shuffled in, dropped his bulk into a chair, and the interviews began.

"When a reporter poses a question, I tell the truth," Delano said. "I don't lie for anybody."

A TV newscaster asked if the same man committed all the rapes that the task force studied.

"Yes," Delano said.

A buzz traveled through the room. The next question was logical: Do you think an innocent man is in jail?

"Yeah," Delano replied.

With that, the next news cycle was underway, and with it tensions erupted between Delano and Clark.

Clark met with Thomas D'Agostino, Capozzi's lawyer, and agreed to share any information that might help his client's cause. But Clark also waged a war of words via the media, stressing adherence to legal procedures.

"People's opinions about Capozzi's innocence are absolutely irrelevant," Clark said. According to the law, he explained, evidence was needed that had not been available at the trial—evidence that might have led to a different verdict had it been known in 1987.

The DA's public comments infuriated Delano, especially because Clark's assistants had been forewarned.

"All I asked was for them to take a look at it," he said. "Suddenly Frank Clark is on TV saying detectives' opinions are irrelevant. What a load of crap. It wasn't an opinion. I had facts to back it up, but nobody ever asked to see the chart. No one had the courtesy to want to know why we felt so strongly about this. Instead of taking an adversarial role, why didn't Frank Clark just say, *I've been made aware of this and we're going to look into it?* His comments made no sense to me."

Delano did not appreciate the slight. As the DA's office became more embroiled with the case, he began to question the propriety of their actions.

"The task force knew stuff that nobody else knew," Delano explained. "When we investigated this case and found it was Sanchez, we only gave the DA what he needed to prosecute. He didn't know about half the things we uncovered to get to that point. It's impossible for him to gather that much information. He was provided enough to get a conviction. We had so much on Sanchez that he was like a trapped rat. There was no way he couldn't admit to being the Bike Path Rapist. He would have been killed in court.

"But the DA manipulated us into reversing roles. They took the investigation away from us and started their own. They told the investigating officers only what we needed to know without giving the whole picture. It's totally improper."

Meanwhile, Anthony Capozzi remained in jail.

Ken Case requested that each phone call Sanchez made or received from the Erie County Holding Center be recorded and burned onto a CD. The attorney wanted to hear any and everything that Sanchez said, whether speaking to friends, Kathleen, or his sons.

Case expected that husband and wife would be in contact regularly, like any longtime couple. But their taped conversations were surprising. Rather than discuss the whirlwind of events that had occurred since Sanchez's arrest, talks were marked by a mundane banality. They never spoke about accusations of rape and murder.

"Kathleen called and they would talk for twenty minutes," Case noted. "But it was strange that not once did he mention why he was jailed. They had a conversation about everyday things, like the furnace at their house, but not about him being arrested. She never asked, and he never volunteered. It was like they would talk about anything except the most important issue."

Drmacich, the neighbor whose family remains close to Kathleen Sanchez, agreed that Al had a tendency to avoid uncomfortable discussions with his wife.

"Kathy got sick of him acting like the ordinary husband after his arrest. He'd call and ask how things are at the house, chitchatting and avoiding the elephant in the room. He pretended everything was normal and fine."

Whether he was in a state of denial or truly believed he could beat the charges, Sanchez retained his easygoing demeanor even behind bars. The holding center's third floor houses a cell under twenty-four-hour observation. Nicknamed "Charlie Constant Obs," the room has a Plexiglas divide overlooking a square space with four bunks. Approximately the size of a classroom, juveniles and prisoners who might be threatened spend time here.[22] Without access to TV or other amenities, there is little to do but whittle away hours in solace.

Ryan Garra, a teenager from the village of Blasdell, spent several weeks in lockup, two beds away from Sanchez. Only after he was released in the spring of 2007 did Garra realize that the brooding prisoner he called "Al" was the notorious Bike Path Rapist.

"When you're in jail, you don't talk about why you're there because others can use that against you to get their sentences reduced," Garra said. "Still, we had conversations all day because there wasn't anything else to do. We chatted about working, jobs we had had, life in general. He always talked about the Bible. His wife brought him a Bible with Old and New Testaments and he read that thing front to back and back to front. When he wasn't reading it, he'd ask if anyone else wanted to and passed it along."

Garra considered his fellow cellmate a "nice guy." Although he never witnessed any display of temper, Garra sensed that Sanchez had a nasty streak that could be switched on and off.

"He was just a quiet, laid-back person, someone I could go to for help. He wondered why somebody so

---

[22] While in custody at the Erie County Holding Center, Sanchez was attacked by a fellow prisoner on June 22, 2007. A 38-year-old Tonawanda resident recognized Sanchez, asked his name, then punched him in the face, causing bruises and cuts.

"He's a raping son of a bitch and he kills women," the attacker told sheriffs. "I hit him. Do what you want to me."

young as me was in jail. I told him it was a bunch of bull. I said my problems should blow over and be dismissed due to evidence."

Sanchez's reply was telling.

"Evidence can be a good or bad thing, depending on what it is," he said.

Evidence against Sanchez was damning. He was clearly connected to the murders of Linda Yalem and Majane Mazur. The link to Joan Diver's homicide, however, was tenuous from a legal standpoint. Although there was little doubt he was responsible, no evidence was found on or around her body that could be used by the prosecution. The droplet of sweat discovered inside her SUV remained a quagmire.

At the pre-trial hearing, defense attorney Andrew LoTempio, representing Sanchez, said his client would plead guilty to the Yalem and Mazur murders, but not Diver. Sanchez remained steadfast that he was not involved with her death.

"I said to his lawyer, police worked backward and found your client through that murder," Case recalled. "The similarities were overwhelming: the bike path, a ligature, the anniversary of Yalem's death, Joan Diver's clothes being removed the same way."

Case told LoTempio, "Give me twelve jurors and I'll take my chances. We'll nail him for that one too."

LoTempio considered before replying, "I'll bring that information back to my client."

Task force detectives remained troubled, however. There was no definitive legal proof that Sanchez had killed Diver. Case shared the officers' commitment to link the killer with his final victim. The investigation would continue. Work needed to be done before the connection would stick.

Case's boss, however, appeared unconcerned. According to Case, he talked with Frank Clark in the DA's office to explain the situation.

"Good enough," Clark said with a shrug.

"What do you mean?" Case asked. "We've got to prosecute on Joan Diver."

"Who cares?" Clark said, waving a dismissive hand. "Sanchez will get fifty years to life and die in prison."

Case was stunned at the ambivalence. He felt as if walls were collapsing around him. Swallowing, he repeated his boss's words, indignation creeping into his voice amid efforts to remain calm.

"Who cares? I think the people in the community will care. I think Steven Diver, who is the father of four children he now has to raise on his own, will care that we go after his wife's killer."

Clark studied the assistant standing before him. An extra quarter century for a fifty-year-old man given a fifty-year sentence would make no difference. Rage rose in Clark's neck. He did not tolerate subordinates questioning his decisions. Face flushed, he stood and pounded a fist against the flat desktop.

"I don't give a fuck about Steven Diver!" Clark screamed, the Ted Kennedy accent dripping from his lips.

Case watched the man rail, his heartbeat pounding, draped in disbelief. *What has Steven Diver ever done to him,* he wondered. Slowly, with blood boiling, Case turned and walked the hall toward his office in silence.

Once inside, Case closed the door and exhaled loudly. The moment was surreal. The district attorney, elected to prosecute criminals, had chosen to ignore a high-profile murder that gained national media attention and polarized the community. A fellow prosecutor who overheard the exchange said ominously, "This is the most dysfunctional office I've ever seen."

Not long afterward, Case resigned his post with the DA's office.[23]

---

[23] Case took a job with the New York State Committee on Judicial Conduct. In April 2008, he announced candidacy for District Attorney, planning to run against his former boss. Although his name did not appear on the Democratic ballot in the November 2008 elections because he lost the primary, during the campaign he received endorsements from several law enforcement organizations.

The Miracle

As weeks stretched to months after Sanchez's arrest, Delano found himself treading in quicksand. The serial killer was captured, but an innocent man still wallowed in jail. In spite of his efforts, every attempt to reverse the fate of Anthony Capozzi slammed into a dead end. Without convincing evidence to overturn his conviction, the best anyone could hope for was that Capozzi be paroled at his next hearing, scheduled for April 2007.

Because he refused to admit guilt or express remorse, Capozzi had been denied parole five times since his sentence. Delano hoped that the findings of the task force would provide a reasonable doubt, allowing the board to reconsider its hardened stance.

"Capozzi was convicted based on the eyewitness testimony of two victims," Delano stated. "The case was purely circumstantial. But those same conditions did not apply when it came to his release. The DA required hard evidence to turn him loose."

The injustice was not lost on Delano or the Capozzi family, who remained advocates for Anthony.

"It's easier to put a man in jail than it is to get one out," Delano lamented.

Side by side photos of Sanchez and Capozzi from twenty-five years earlier show two men who appear strikingly similar. Both have round faces, black hair, dark eyes, and thin mustaches. Any witness might confuse one for the other. Without identification, it is difficult to tell the men apart even after studying the photos. The rape victims had only a passing glance under emotional duress.

"I knew Capozzi was innocent just by the paper-work," Delano said. "That's what was so frustrating. Everybody else was urging us to find some kind of evidence. We couldn't locate DNA slides, but it was clear he didn't do these rapes. At the very minimum, there were enough circumstantial factors to grant him parole."

If proof was needed to overturn Capozzi's conviction, from where would that proof magically appear? Investigators sought rape kits, which contain medical evidence gathered within hours of an attack. When a victim seeks professional treatment, a nurse performs a vaginal wash and swab, combing for stray hairs left by an attacker. Evidence slides are saved in the rape kit, which is given to authorities for storage.

"Nurses know how to do the procedure," Savage explained. "They put everything into a box, seal it with evidence tape, then hand it to the investigating officer."

Few rape kits were saved after the five-year statute of limitations expired. From a legal standpoint, they would be useless, only gobbling up space. So after an allotted amount of time has passed, blood and semen samples are often discarded.

"Many police departments have evidence that piles up," Savage explained. "It becomes a huge management

issue. Where do you store it? How do you keep track of
it? Some of the serological samples have to be sealed in
a polymer slide or even refrigerated. After seven or ten
years go by, police departments say, what are we saving
this evidence for? Even if we find out who did the rape, he
can't be prosecuted for it. So it gets destroyed."

Different jurisdictions have different policies, however, and there is no standard timetable. Sometimes samples are thrown away during sporadic cleaning sprees or
when office space needs to be rearranged.

A series of concurrent events fell in line, allowing
detectives to uncover long-buried slides. Delano calls
this the miracle that freed Capozzi.

On July 7, 1977, a girl in a community south of Buffalo
rode her bicycle along a road that paralleled Lake Erie
and noticed a van following her. It would speed up, slow
down, then disappear. As she rounded a bend, a young
man stood before the van's open hood, tinkering with the
engine. Short and stocky, he sought directions to a nearby
beach. She pointed west and started to pedal away, but
he sprinted ahead, knocking her off balance before dragging her into the brush and raping her.

Only a teenager at the time, she contacted authorities to report the attack. No suspect was found, and the
incident grew cold until nearly thirty years later. After
the Bike Path Rapist's high-profile arrest, the grown
woman saw Sanchez's picture and phoned Delano. She
was adamant that Sanchez was the man who raped her
nearly three decades before.

"This would have been right after he graduated high school, before the Delaware Park rapes," Delano noted. "It happened in Lake View but she couldn't remember which police department she called. It might have been Hamburg or Evans or someplace else. No one could locate her report."

The woman was frustrated by the missing paperwork, worrying that Delano thought she was simply concocting a story.

"I planned to meet with her, take a statement and try to find those files," Delano said.

A detective from Evans, Samuel DeJohn, also expressed interest in the case, believing it was connected to an unsolved rape in his jurisdiction. In that attack, a young girl was raped and beaten. The man wore a construction hat and used a toy cap gun to accost his victim.

"I thought it was a long shot that his case was the Bike Path Rapist," Delano recalled. "He never used a toy gun and in general he didn't beat the hell out of women. He was using a ligature. Nothing matched except the fact there was a rape in the woods."

In the weeks following Sanchez's arrest, Amherst detective Ed Monan collaborated with DeJohn, trying to link the unsolved assault to the Bike Path Rapist. Although the statute of limitations had expired, investigators wanted to close out as many cases as possible. Since Joan Diver's murder, Sanchez had been connected to more attacks than originally thought. Perhaps additional rapes could be proven as well.

Because no one could locate the victim's paperwork, DeJohn and Monan went to visit her one wintry morning. En route to the interview, DeJohn complained about old slides being discarded. Evans police had no physical proof to connect any attacks to Sanchez.

Monan suggested contacting the Erie County Medical Center in Buffalo. Victims raped within the city were often examined there, so perhaps some evidence remained in storage.

Task force officers had been asking the same questions. At the command center on Oak Street, Delano's cubicle was adjacent to Lissa Redmond's. They often yelled to each other over the dividers. Banter went back and forth as Delano asked, "Did you call the hospital today?"

Both detectives had regularly phoned ECMC's morgue trying to track down evidence. Prior to investigating the Bike Path case, Delano had dealt with ECMC while working a thirty-three-year-old murder case, so he was familiar with the slow pace of unearthing files.

"We kept bugging these people, saying you must have these slides," Delano recalled. "We didn't want to encounter any lazy workers. Some people might tell you they looked for stuff but couldn't find it, when in fact they never looked. So we just kept nagging them."

Delano finally contacted the chief medical examiner.

"Doc," he said, "they tell me the slides are destroyed but I find that hard to believe."

"No, they must be here somewhere," came the response. "I'll personally look for them."

But when he called back a few days later, it confirmed what others had said: Old evidence was discarded because of the statute of limitations.

DeJohn, however, did manage to discover one slide in question. He had spoken to Ann Victor Lazarous, who worked at the hospital and knew that slides were stored in the pathology department. Prior to this, queries had gone to other departments, not pathology.

"Lissa and I had been calling the hospital, and they were telling us no such thing existed," Delano said. "But when I asked DeJohn if he found that old paperwork, he told me I should contact the pathology department at ECMC because they located a slide from his girl. Maybe there were still files from the Delaware Park rapes."

DeJohn had learned that the hospital had stored thirty years worth of slides, stretching from 1973 to 2002. It was the break that investigators needed.

Delano spoke to Lazarous, who agreed the evidence was most likely buried somewhere in their row of metal cabinets. She asked that a formal request with names and birth dates be submitted on police letterhead. Delano composed a query letter immediately, faxing it within minutes.

"Ann Victor Lazarous knows everything about the hospital," Delano said. "Once we made contact with her, it was gold. From then on, if we needed something, we went straight to her. If she wasn't there, her secretary took care of us. After our first request, we waited for a day or two before she discovered all our slides."

Delano was elated. DNA evidence could now be tested. He was certain that Capozzi had not done the rapes for which he was convicted, and now there would be proof. But why was this evidence only coming to light now, after Capozzi spent twenty-two years in prison?

"It's sad, but the key to Capozzi's freedom had been there for years," Savage admitted. "It's just that nobody knew where to look. One side didn't know the other was searching for it until they finally connected."

Unknown to police, when victims underwent swabbing for a rape kit, another test was given simultaneously.

Hospital personnel also made a slide that was sent to the pathology lab to see if the woman was exposed to any communicable diseases. It was not considered evidence, but patient information. The test was done for sexually transmitted diseases, to see if the victim was in danger and whether antibiotics were needed. That is the reason the swabs were sent to pathology. If results were negative, there was no protocol once the lab finished examining them. They could have been thrown out, but somebody decided to put them in a file cabinet.

"The hospital had no obligation to store these," Delano said. "Technically, they probably shouldn't have because they are confidential patient information. But ECMC has been doing that since the 1970s."

Filing cabinets were filled with thousands of such slides. Open a random drawer, and pull one out to see two pieces of glass pressed together. In the center of the plates, barely visible to the naked eye, is a smear. An attached tag identifies the woman's name.

"The files are stored behind a door and very few people even knew they existed," Delano reflected. "It was a miracle. Those slides were what freed Capozzi. It wouldn't have happened any other way."

But discovering the slides was only a first step. Justice lagged behind, falling victim to closed-door politics.

Once it was established that slides existed, the next step was to have the district attorney issue search warrants for evidence in question. But the DA's office was in no hurry to do that.

"They were dragging their feet, and nobody could tell me why," Delano said. "After jerking us around, we finally got a warrant. Our evidence people picked up the slides and submitted them to the CPS lab."

Included were all the swabs available from the Delaware Park rapes, and four additional cases Delano had examined. The lab moved slowly, just as the DA's office had, and Delano grew impatient with its testing procedures

Hoping to hasten the process, Redmond phoned Frank Sedita, the deputy district attorney, inquiring about the status. She was informed that it would be another six weeks before Dr. John Simich of the Central Police Services lab could examine the slides. Frustrated, Redmond called Delano to commiserate.

"I blew a gasket," Delano recalled. "What the hell? They can't delay this any longer. There's a guy sitting in prison who is innocent!"

Emboldened by Delano's emotion, Redmond phoned Sedita again. Although equally outraged, she made the call rather than Delano, because she could remain calm and reason with the attorney. Dr. Simich happened to be with Sedita, so a deal was struck: The two rapes for which

Capozzi was convicted would have their slides tested at once, if only to silence Delano.

"They didn't believe that Capozzi was innocent," Delano said. "They thought if they ran tests, they could prove me wrong, shut me up, and put this whole issue to rest. Fine by me."

The conversation took place on a Tuesday. Results would be known within a day or two. On Wednesday, Delano phoned Simich around noon.

"John, any word?" he asked.

"No, they're still in the cooker," the doctor replied. "But I should know soon."

"Call me any time, night or day, as soon as you get results," Delano requested.

"I'll run it by Frank Clark first," Simich said.

Delano took a breath. Why was the district attorney part of this equation?

"I had to argue with him," Delano recalled. "Buffalo police submitted the evidence. It's a police services lab. The DA is not supposed to have any control over them. According to protocol, results should be given to the submitting agency, which was us."

Within hours, Delano and the task force were circumvented. DNA results were processed that conclusively proved that Altemio Sanchez, not Anthony Capozzi, had committed the rapes in Delaware Park. Delano kept his phone handy, anxious for information, but no call came. The district attorney sprung into action without informing police.

Thomas D'Agostino, Capozzi's longtime lawyer, was asked to meet with Frank Clark at 3:00 p.m. D'Agostino called Pam Guenther, one of Anthony Capozzi's sisters, and requested she come along. She served as the family spokesperson but did not know what to expect at the face-to-face meeting.

Once everyone was assembled at 25 Delaware Avenue, Clark spoke frankly.

"I want to cut to the chase and tell you why you're here," the DA said. "DNA test results are in and the rapes were not committed by Anthony."

Guenther grew lightheaded; her vision swam. Through tears, she nearly passed out with joy. It was the answer to decades of her family's prayers.

"I knew that Anthony was innocent all along," Guenther reflected. "But for those words to come from the district attorney's mouth, I felt like I was dreaming."

"That information is not to leave this room," Clark cautioned. "You can tell family members, but I don't want you talking to anyone from the task force or the media. Leaking this could jeopardize Anthony's release."

It is unclear how making this information public would have changed the facts of Capozzi's innocence.

"This particular sister, Pam, was the first family member I met from the Capozzis," Delano recalled. "She's a fighter and doesn't pull any punches, so we became friends. During the investigation, she would call me and ask what was going on. I kept her up to date. I don't think it was proper for Frank Clark to tell her to not talk to anybody."

That evening, Guenther gathered the extended Capozzi clan at her home in Amherst to share the good news. While the family celebrated the confirmation of

Anthony's innocence, Guenther's conscience bothered
her. The DA had ordered her not to contact Delano,
but the detective had been instrumental in freeing her
brother. It was not right that he be shut out.

"After everyone left and I settled down, I began to
get angry," Guenther recalled. "Frank Clark was putting
me in a tough spot. Denny Delano was knocking himself
out but I was instructed not to say a word. I felt obligated
to Denny, but at the same time I didn't want anything to
backfire."

After a fitful night when she was too excited to sleep,
she phoned Delano the following morning.

"I got a call from a mole in the DA's office telling
me that the DNA slides were processed," Delano said.
"I was told, *Great job! Anthony is innocent and is going
to be exonerated. But you can't say you heard from me
or I'll get fired.* In the middle of that conversation, my
cell started beeping. It was Pam, saying she felt terrible
because Frank Clark told her not to talk to me."

"This is horrible because you've always been up front
with my family," she confided.

Delano, overjoyed by the news of Capozzi's impend-
ing freedom, was not about to hold a grudge. He
admitted he had already heard the news and offered
congratulations.

Delano remains puzzled by the district attorney's
actions, especially because Clark was not involved in the
original case in the 1980s, so there would be no personal
shame to admitting a mistake was made.

"When slides came back to Sanchez, not Anthony
Capozzi, Clark stalled for nearly a week before releasing

that information," Delano noted. "It's too dangerous
for one person to have that much authority. But he put
himself into a bad position. The DA sends assistants to
conduct investigations and has full control of the lab
and monitors who submits evidence and who picks it
up. Under Clark's rule, there are no checks and balances.
What if one of those slides wants to get lost?

"I'm not saying the DA's office did anything illegal,
but at the very least, there are ethical questions. No one
is checking them, and they should be held to a higher
standard. Frank Clark was a power freak who wanted to
keep his grip on the office so he got himself on the news
every day instead of focusing on doing the right thing."[24]

At 11:00 a.m. on Wednesday, March 28, Clark held a
press conference to announce DNA findings and address
Capozzi's coming exoneration. As the media scribbled
furiously, confident this story would dominate headlines
for days to come, Clark was the sole official before the
TV cameras. No one from the task force or any other law
enforcement agency was invited.

---

[24] In the spring of 2008, Frank Clark announced he would retire at the end of
his term the following January, citing medical reasons.

Exoneration

Within days, the Capozzi family became celebrities in Western New York. Their story unfolded like an epic from the Old Testament, marked by false accusations and decades of despair. Ultimately a team of cops served up the long overdue redemption. With Anthony's prison release detailed by the media, the Capozzis suddenly became everyone's favorite neighbor. The heartwarming reunion with a long-lost son interested strangers and casual observers.

"Anybody who meets this family immediately falls in love with them," Delano noted. "They're the nicest people I've ever known."

Albert Sr. and Mary Capozzi produced five children. Anthony was the second child and oldest boy. Others include Sharyn Miller, Kathy Jeras, Pam Guenther, and Albert Jr. Mary, the matriarch, leads the clan.

Spirituality has always been a centerpiece in Mary Capozzi's life. When Anthony was led away by authorities on September 13, 1985, and convicted of rape sixteen months later, she never abandoned faith. In the face of adversity, her belief in God only strengthened her commitment.

Mary Capozzi is petite, with tightly curled hair and bright eyes. In her seventies, she exudes a confidence borne from years of torment. Any mother's nightmare is to see her son suffer; Anthony's imprisonment was a greater tragedy because Mary was convinced of his innocence. Daily prayer fortified her. A devout Catholic, she visited Holy Angels Church seven days a week for more than two decades. Each time, in the solace of the sanctuary, she never questioned God's will, instead praying that her son's plight be resolved.

"How could I ask *Why did you do this to me?*" she mused, with the soothing aura of one who is at peace with the world. "I knew God was going to take care of it. He didn't say when, but you have to believe. I prayed every day for twenty-two years. Before I close my eyes for good, I wanted my son home."

Albert Sr. is a handsome man with a square head and thick white hair. He felt shame while his son was jailed, often wondering if Anthony had committed rape. Although his wife's confidence never wavered, Albert was less convinced. A healthy Anthony would never attack a woman, he knew, but his son was plagued by schizophrenia. Perhaps, just perhaps, the boy had done such awful things.

"I lost all faith," Albert admitted. "I never asked him if he did it because I didn't want to know if it was true."

"I knew Anthony couldn't do it," Mary said, waving a dismissive hand. Due to his illness, he could not make simple decisions, so there was no way her son could plan and execute a series of brutal attacks.

Albert's thick body leaned back and he turned reflec-
tive. His wife, he said softly, kept him strong throughout
the ordeal.

After Anthony was convicted, the family bonds
tightened. All the children remained in Buffalo so they
could support their parents and one another. Although
jailed, Anthony became the centerpiece of their lives.
Albert Sr. and Mary visited their son at least once a
week, driving four hundred miles round trip to Marcy
State Prison near Utica during his incarceration there.
They would wake at 6:00 a.m., pack sandwiches, and be
on the road early, leaving them ample time to spend with
Anthony. When Mary was not with him, She frequently
wrote letters to her son narrating ordinary occurrences
around the house.

"I just talked about everyday things. Dad and I are
watching TV right now," she recalled as an example. It
was important to keep him aware of what was happening
in their home. She paused before framing the context of
her commitment. "We had five kids and with only four
there, something was missing."

Old footage from the 1980s shows Anthony Capozzi
in his late twenties, bulky and out of shape, with dark hair,
a narrow mustache, and long sideburns. At his 1987 trial,
Anthony did not understand what was happening around
him. Handcuffed while wearing a blue-gray sweater vest
and open-collared shirt, he displayed a confused expression, mouth agape. He often smiled at TV cameras. In the
context of grave rape accusations, his friendly demeanor
appeared sinister, lending him a guilty air.

Capozzi's involvement with the Delaware Park rapes was a fluke, a misfortune of his resemblance to Altemio Sanchez. William Buyers, then the city's commissioner of human resources, encountered a suspicious man in the park in July of 1984. The next day, a rape occurred near that spot. When details of the attack were made public, Buyers told officers he had seen the rapist and provided a description. He promised to alert authorities if he noticed the man again.

Fourteen months later, at a Perkins Restaurant on Delaware Avenue, Buyers spotted him, copied down his license number, and phoned in a tip.

But he identified the wrong person. Four detectives visited Capozzi's home the evening of September 12, 1985. They searched for the rapist's clothing as described by a victim: maroon shorts and a yellow tank top. They also looked for a gun.

The Capozzi family was confused, but not worried.

"My son never wore shorts or a tank top because he had a lot of hair on his arms and legs and was self-conscious about it," Mary explained. Because she did the household laundry, she was confident Anthony did not have the clothes that officers sought.

Nothing incriminating was found, but the next morning, officers returned and took Anthony into custody. Two rape victims had identified him as their attacker. As her son was led away, Mary stood on the front porch weeping, but Anthony reassured her he had done nothing wrong and would return soon.

He spent the next twenty-two years locked up. In spite of his mental illness, he never admitted guilt, although doing so might have hastened his parole. Family members suggested he make a confession, even if it was false. It would mean he had a better chance at returning home.

"I didn't do it and I'm not going to admit it," Anthony said adamantly.

Like a Greek tragedy, misfortune fell in line before Capozzi.

Photos from the time show his physical resemblance to Sanchez was unnerving. Although Capozzi is eighteen months older, they looked virtually the same age. Both men had a round face, thin mustache, and dark eyes. The rapist, however, was thought to weigh 150 pounds, while Capozzi was above 200. Capozzi also sported a scar on his forehead, the result of an altercation in the early 1980s in which he had been thrown through a plate-glass window. None of the rape victims mentioned this feature when describing their attacker.

Dr. Howard C. Wilinsky, a forensic psychiatrist, examined Capozzi after the arrest. He diagnosed a paranoid schizophrenic disorder, and wrote a letter to Capozzi's attorney.

"His condition is such that, in my opinion, Mr. Capozzi would have been unable to carry out the acts as they are alleged to have occurred on December 14, 1983, April 2, 1984, and July 8, 1984," it stated.

Wilinsky was to have been a key defense witness. However, emergency surgery derailed that plan before the trial began. The doctor was unable to testify on Capozzi's behalf.

Further rapes occurred in Delaware Park while Capozzi was locked in the Erie County Holding Center. At the urging of the prosecution, the judge did not allow those to be mentioned in court.

Before DNA evidence proved Capozzi's innocence, Delano probed another possible avenue toward exoneration. Capozzi, he learned, had been a patient at the Buffalo Psychiatric Center from December 1983 to March 1984. Two of the rapes for which Capozzi was accused occurred during this time. This could be the magic ticket. If he was being cared for at the Psych Center, how could he have committed rapes?

But even this was not conclusive. Capozzi had not been under twenty-four-hour watch, Delano learned. He could have been unsupervised for blocks of time, his whereabouts unknown. It was nearly impossible to find anyone who could testify to Anthony's location during specific times when the rapes occurred because twenty-three years had passed.

"Everything that could go wrong for Anthony did go wrong," Delano recalled. "The case against him was purely circumstantial."

After being informed by the district attorney that her brother was innocent, Pam Guenther invited the family to her Amherst home that evening. Many had bought tickets for a fund-raiser at Williamsville East High

School, where Guenther's son is a student. In fact, in all the excitement, she had to cook ten pounds of pasta for the benefit.

She had kept the good news under wraps for several hours because she was reluctant to tell one family member before another. Rather than repeat her tale several times, she brought everyone together to share the unexpected turn. While her mother and father sat at the kitchen table and her brother, sisters, and their various children gathered around, she asked, "What's the best news I could give you?" When everyone muttered Anthony's name, she said, "Well, our wish has just come true."

After learning Anthony had been wrongly convicted, initial disbelief was followed by euphoria. Tears flowed freely; people jumped and hugged. Words were inadequate to express the cascade of emotions.

"Have you ever felt pure joy in your heart?" Albert Sr. asked. At that moment, he knew he would die in peace because his son had been vindicated.

The next day, Wednesday, March 28, 2007, the family assembled at a hair salon on Main Street in Williamsville, owned by Kathy Jeras, Anthony's younger sister. Together, they listened to a live radio broadcast of the district attorney explaining Anthony's exoneration. While reporters and TV cameras crowded into the shop and chronicled their reactions, Albert and Mary sat on a sofa surrounded by their children. It was a surreal event.

Using a cell phone, they contacted Anthony, still incarcerated at Attica Prison.

Sharyn Miller, Anthony's older sister, basked in the moment. That day she asked what was the tallest building in Buffalo, because she wanted to stand atop it and shout to the world that her brother was innocent.

"You're free, Ant," Miller bellowed to her brother into the phone, voice cracking with emotion. "You're free. They realized you didn't do any of those things. You're free. They made a mistake."

There was a pause before Anthony responded, "That sounds good to me."

Laughter was flecked with tears.

Mary Capozzi took the phone from her daughter. "Anthony, you're finally coming home, honey," she said.

For the first time, Anthony grasped what he was being told. His voice brimmed with excitement.

"Really?"

The joy was tempered by the price paid for lost time. Could the amount of Anthony's suffering ever be quantified? Missing years washed away the possibility for a normal life with a wife and children. Had he been free, perhaps he would have found the right doctor, and secured a combination of medicines that allowed him to function and contribute to society. Now, at age fifty, Anthony had surrendered those experiences. There was concern for his present mental health. After decades behind bars, had he been treated properly?

"When you go to state prison, it's not like you're getting the best psychological care," Greg Savage observed. "They medicate inmates to keep them under control. If it wasn't for his family, Capozzi never would have survived. They kept him connected to the world."

Many wondered how he would function after being institutionalized for so long. A plan was crafted to utilize outpatient services and continue strong family support.

But before that could occur, Capozzi needed to be released. Word came that the process might take up to thirty days. Many in the community were outraged.

"Thirty days?" Delano wondered, voice rising with disgust. "The guy is innocent. He doesn't belong there another minute. Just release him. I wanted to go down to pick him up myself."

As the Capozzi story flooded the Western New York airwaves, a judge phoned a radio talk show and suggested there was a way to expedite the process. Armed with this information, Delano dropped hints in the media urging fast action. A hearing was held on Monday, and by Tuesday, April 3, Capozzi was a free man after more than two decades.

While the Capozzis celebrated, friends and acquaintances professed their long-held belief in Anthony's innocence. Neighbors wrapped giant blue bows around the trees in front of the Capozzis' home on Jersey Street to welcome Anthony back.

Not everyone, however, shared the elation. Armed with the proof he had clamored for three months earlier, district attorney Frank Clark tempered the enthusiasm in somber tones.

"Obviously, this is a situation which has both joy and sorrow," he said at a news conference. "Joy is obviously because an innocent man has been vindicated. The sad part is that he has spent twenty years in jail before that happened."

Erie County judge Sheila DiTullio had prosecuted the case while a member of the DA's office in 1987. Transcripts from court proceedings on September 19, 1985, reveal that a juror was puzzled because technology was not being utilized to ensure the right man was in custody. The juror asked if any tests had been done comparing Capozzi's blood to the sperm samples culled from rape victims. DiTullio answered no.

"That's not a normal practice?" the juror persisted.

"I can't answer that now, but I'll say not in this case," DiTullio replied.

Two days after Capozzi's release, DiTullio released a statement of apology.

"I deeply regret the outcome of this case," she said. "I realize it brings little comfort or consolation to Mr. Capozzi or his family. I handled this case fairly and honestly based on all the evidence and information that was available at the time. This is the most troubling and upsetting circumstance in my twenty-five years as a lawyer and judge."

Even more haunted, however, were the victims who had positively identified Capozzi as their attacker once he was seized into custody in 1985. During a follow-up interview in 2007, one woman admitted she may have been mistaken by choosing him from a lineup, but a different victim insisted that it was Capozzi who had raped her. When DNA evidence proved otherwise, she was devastated.

"She passed out on the kitchen floor," Delano said. "Until then she was adamant and would not back off. She was certain Capozzi was her attacker because of the way he walked."

The victim has since sought forgiveness from the Capozzi family. With a priest serving as an intermediary, she composed a letter to Mary Capozzi and offered a quilt that she knitted herself.

Before this case, Delano had not met the Capozzis, nor had he ever heard of Anthony's plight. But during the legal quagmire to free him, the ties became intense. Delano and his wife have shared meals at the Capozzis' home and even celebrated Easter together.

"The first time I saw Denny Delano he was on TV talking to the media," Pam Guenther said. "He claimed the wrong man was in jail. I called my mom and said 'Do you believe what he's saying? There is a detective who believes Anthony isn't a rapist. I love this guy.'"

Long after the case has ended, the bonds between Delano and the Capozzis remain strong. Knowing how much Albert Sr. values his wife and children, his words convey a powerful meaning.

"He's family," Albert Sr. said simply.

Guilty

While battling for Anthony Capozzi's exoneration, the task force's primary job was to find a way that Sanchez could be prosecuted for the Diver homicide. After the rapist's capture, the task force quickly changed shape. Although investigators from Amherst and the state police withdrew by the end of January, a core group remained at Oak Street for several months. Unsolved rapes around Western New York were probed with hope of discovering any additional open files that matched the killer's pattern and m.o.

Several promising leads emerged on further rapes. With images of Altemio Sanchez flooding the media, women came forward from years past, some who had been raped and others who eluded their attacker but were convinced that Sanchez had tried to accost them.

As stories began to trickle into the task force office, investigators realized there were probably scores of unreported incidents. How many attacks had Sanchez attempted? He may have been responsible for many, but there was no definitive way to prove them all.

"The case ended and everybody wanted to go home," Delano explained. "But had we worked longer, we would have uncovered more victims. No question. We've got women who describe him perfectly, but there is no DNA evidence to link him. I had a girl call me who said she was camping out of state and was attacked. It fits his m.o. perfectly. But she never got a rape kit. I know he had other victims."

The most intriguing case to surface was an unsolved murder in Kenmore. There, on July 1, 1985, the body of a fifteen-year-old girl was discovered lying on a railroad track near the Buffalo border. After several months of dead-end investigations, the crime went cold for more than twenty years until Sanchez's arrest. Suddenly, a fresh connection appeared. Was it a coincidence that the scene was only a half-mile from American Brass, the factory where the killer had worked? Was there a link because he had attacked girls along these same railroad tracks before?

Many wondered if the teenager, Katherine Herold, was a victim of the serial rapist. If so, this would have been Sanchez's first murder, five years before Linda Yalem was strangled.

Herold's father had been the Buffalo Museum of Science director, and a professor at Buffalo State College. At the time of her murder, Herold was a freshman at Kenmore West High School. Her father had died of a heart attack the year before, and this affected her deeply. In the wake of his death, her personality changed. She began to rebel, staying out late and making new friends in a rough crowd.

After telling her mother she was meeting classmates at a local park, Herold's body was discovered by a train crew the following morning. Lying on the tracks, she wore a white sweater and jeans. There was a cut over one eye, and something had been pressed into her neck hard enough to cause a red indentation.

Almost twenty-two years later, in the spring of 2007, Town of Tonawanda detectives reviewed the case, noting similarities between it and crimes committed by the Bike Path Rapist. Members of the task force were contacted and officers from different jurisdictions poured over evidence together. Opinions are mixed as to whether Sanchez was responsible for this homicide.[25]

Delano insists that Sanchez did not murder Kathy Herold. In this instance, he believes the killer is telling the truth when he denies knowledge of her death.

"It wasn't him," Delano stated. "I can't seem to convince other people, but I'm confident Sanchez didn't do this."

Before reaching this conclusion, Delano studied the complete case file. He believes the differences between Sanchez's other crimes and this one are clear enough to be obvious.

"I read enough of the cases that Sanchez did do," Delano explained. "He has a certain method of behavior. Many factors in his attacks are the same. When one comes along that he didn't do, it sticks out.

"It's a no-brainer on the surface, but when you dig into it, things become even more evident. First of all, she was found on the railroad tracks fully dressed. That's

---

[25] From prison, Sanchez has repeatedly denied any involvement. It should be noted that until evidence connected him to Joan Diver's murder, he refused to admit he killed her as well.

not him. She wasn't sexually assaulted. That's not him, because that was his whole thing. He confronted girls for sex. At the very least he would have ripped her bra off. She was also beaten in the face. That's a giveaway. He didn't beat anybody."

Crime scene photos revealed a mark on Herold's neck. Some investigators believe it resembled the brush burn on Joan Diver's cheek, inflicted during the struggle to wrap the ligature over her head. Delano used a magnifying glass before asserting that Herold's scar did not originate from a rope or wire garrote.

"By the time the police photographer arrived on the scene to take pictures, somebody had moved her body off the railroad track," Delano explained. "That mark came from lying against the edge of the track all night. It's not a ligature scar."

In spite of his explanations, Delano remains a vocal minority. He cannot convince fellow officers, some of whom believe this was Sanchez's first experiment with murder.

Scott Patronik remains unsure.

"That's a tough one," he reflected. "We met with Tonawanda detectives and reviewed evidence. The things that hit me are how many coincidences can you have? She was found on railroad tracks, yards from where Sanchez works. He strangled people who fought and this girl had a reputation as a fighter. The scars on her neck look like ligature marks, but they may be caused by the placement of the body on the tracks. I'm still not sure one way or the other."

*

While authorities were confident that Sanchez had killed Joan Diver, solid evidence did not exist linking him to the crime scene. The only connection was the droplet of sweat containing his DNA that had been found on the steering wheel of Diver's SUV. Neither the crime scene nor her body contained any proof that Sanchez had been there.

Because of this, the district attorney's office was reluctant to proceed with a murder charge. While they indicted on the Yalem and Mazur homicides, something more was needed—a witness, or newfound evidence— before Sanchez could be charged for Diver's death. The break that linked him to his last murder came from an unlikely source.

Sheriff's deputy Rick Lauricella was leaving supplies at a Salvation Army drop-off site a few weeks after Sanchez's capture when he encountered a family friend working there. Lauricella chatted with the sixty-nine-year-old woman. Knowing he was a cop, she steered the conversation to the Bike Path Rapist, which continued to play heavily in the media.

"You know, it's funny," she said. "When I saw him on TV after his arrest, I remembered that guy. I sold him a piece of cable back when I worked at Hector's Hardware."

This exchange was relayed back to Alan Rozansky, who was the lead investigator on the Diver murder. He had been pursuing several angles to connect Sanchez to that crime, but none had proved successful. Rozansky believed the new information could be important.

"How do you know the guy you sold cable to is Altemio Sanchez?" he asked, after setting up a face-to-face meeting with the witness.

"I'm 100 percent sure that was him," she answered, agreeing to testify if necessary.

A representative from the district attorney's office took a statement, then she, Rozansky and assistant district attorney Ken Case returned to the hardware store on Main Street in Clarence where she had recently been employed. She pointed out the type of wire she remembered selling to Sanchez.

"I showed him the wire that goes to lamps and stereos and he said no to this type," she recalled. "We went back to the spool of cable. He purchased two four-foot pieces. I thought it was strange that he was only buying four feet because most people buy forty or fifty feet."

The transaction occurred in the morning sometime during the last week of September, only days before Diver was strangled. The cord cost sixty cents, and he paid cash.

"I saw him on television after his arrest and my mouth dropped open and I got a chill up my spine," the woman recalled. "I had been so close to him."

Experts from the Erie County morgue examined the twisted spiral pattern of the cable and matched it to imprints on Joan Diver's neck. They could say with certainty that the cord was the same type used to strangle her.

"Once we had that piece of cable and a witness, the DA's office said they could now indict on Diver," Rozansky recalled. "Until that point, everything was circumstantial, but this put it over the edge."

The former hardware store clerk testified before a grand jury, and on Thursday, March 1, Sanchez was indicted for a third murder.

In spite of overwhelming evidence, Sanchez continued to deny he was the Bike Path Rapist. During the initial interview in January, he told investigators he did not know how his DNA was discovered on so many women. He could not say more, he insisted, because he knew nothing about it. From the Erie County Holding Center, he hired Andrew LoTempio, a well-known defense lawyer in Western New York, to provide legal representation.

During the next several months, LoTempio reviewed the case against his client. The evidence overwhelmingly pointed toward Sanchez. The attorney suggested an insanity plea, recognizing there was no chance for an acquittal.

On Wednesday, May 16, Sanchez shuffled into a courtroom packed with family members of those he murdered. One former rape victim kept vigil as well. Shackled around the wrists and ankles, he wore a charcoal suit and maroon tie. Observers anticipated a series of mundane legal motions regarding his upcoming trial. But when addressed by State Supreme Court justice

Christopher Burns, Sanchez's words stunned the somber audience. For the first time, he admitted what had already been proved.

He was the Bike Path Rapist.

When the judge asked how he killed Linda Yalem, Sanchez muttered, "I strangled her." He confessed the same thing about Majane Mazur.

While those in the courtroom found the confession unexpected, Kathleen Sanchez, sitting with her brother in the second row, anticipated what was coming. Since his arrest in January, he had maintained the façade of innocence with his family. But as the case steamrolled against Sanchez, he recognized there was no evading the law this time. There would be a trial, and he would be found guilty. At the urging of his attorney, Sanchez reluctantly confided in his wife, however belatedly. Until that point, Kathleen had championed his innocence.

Later that day, the lawyer suggested that Sanchez confessed in court to spare his wife and children the spectacle of a high-profile trial and the expected media circus. Undoubtedly, lurid and gruesome details would be unearthed, and every aspect of the Sanchez family would be scrutinized. Admitting guilt in this venue was a way to shield his loved ones.

Delano believes this theory is a convenient public relations spin.

"I saw what he did to people," Delano noted. "I don't understand how he could love his wife and kids if that's what he thought of human life. This guy had no sense of remorse, period. The women he raped and killed were not human beings as far as he was concerned, so I don't buy that he was trying to spare someone's feelings. He confessed because we had him."

"Sexual gratification was the number one thing in his life and everything else was secondary," agreed Alan Rozansky. "Truth was secondary. Family was secondary. Everything took a backseat to his sexual urges."

The question remained: How could Sanchez have been a serial rapist and murderer for so long without his wife being aware of what he did?

"Law enforcement in this community went almost thirty years without putting two and two together," LoTempio told the media that day. "So it's not out of this world that she wouldn't either."

In court, as her husband admitted to being the long-sought serial killer, Kathleen Sanchez wept and squeezed her brother's arm. After his guilty plea, her lawyer released a brief statement expressing condolences to victims. It read:

"It is unimaginable to us that someone we have truly loved and respected so much for so many years could be capable of such violent acts, and we are sincerely sorry and filled with grief for your tragic losses."

Sentencing

As the sun ascended on Tuesday, August 14, 2007, the buildings of downtown Buffalo cast shadows that ebbed from Lake Erie's shore. The morning dawned bright with hope. A gentle breeze swept away lingering humidity. Men and women swung briefcases and shoulder bags when crossing city streets, bustling toward offices.

Ordinary to some, but to others, it was a day of reckoning. After nearly thirty years of evasion, a serial rapist and killer faced justice.

Sentencing was originally scheduled for early August, but proceedings were delayed two weeks to accommodate a victim's relative living out of town, who was unable to attend on the initial date.

Strict security is the norm at the Erie County Courthouse, a tall rectangular building on the northeast corner of Church Street and Delaware Avenue. Armed officers scrutinize everyone entering the lobby. Much like an airport, visitors pass through metal detectors while their belongings are scanned atop a conveyor belt.

Sentencing was to commence at 9:30 a.m., and more than an hour earlier news vans began clustering nearby. Cameramen assembled on the sidewalk, while reporters from rival stations smoked cigarettes, idly engaging in gossip. Some passed through security and descended one floor to wait in a cramped lobby outside the basement courtroom.

At 8:40 a.m., cameras rolled as Kathleen Sanchez, dressed in a gray suit, entered the foyer. Her brother, a muscular man with a shaved head wearing a blue dress shirt and tie, escorted her like a bodyguard. His intimidating stature dwarfed an accompanying couple, relegating them to the background. Kathleen's expression was stoic, as if resigned to coming pain. Voices hushed as she passed; one TV personality sought her cameraman's attention and stabbed the air, signaling that he film Kathleen's entrance.

Across the street from the courthouse is the Erie County Holding Center. Alan Rozansky stood on its concrete stoop wearing a dress uniform—short-sleeve black shirt with a silver star on the breast, and black trousers. A contented grin spread across his face. Although the courthouse was cast in shadow, sunlight blanketed him as he watched the gathering from the bright side of Delaware Avenue. He paused long enough to consider the tangled course this case had undergone, ruminating on the frustrations and setbacks before the puzzle pieces finally snapped into place. Rozansky knew this was a day to savor. There had been important busts before, but the Bike Path Rapist's capture signaled a defining moment in his career.

The basement courtroom was selected because only one door led inside and a narrow hallway opened onto an elevator. The location was secure, off the beaten path. Visitors would not stumble in by accident.

A phalanx of deputies posted watch before the wooden doors while the press assembled anxiously. Kathleen Sanchez and her associates were ushered inside, as were various police officers. Josh Keats, sporting a freshly trimmed crew cut, shook hands with guards as they allowed him to pass. At 9:00 a.m., doors were propped open and reporters rushed in.

It was a large, drab room, L-shaped with eggshell-colored walls, overhead fluorescent lights, and seating for more than one hundred. A railing divided the gallery from the prosecutor's and defendant's tables.

The first several rows were reserved for law enforcement. Sheriff's officers in matching black clustered together, talking in muted tones. Led by Erie County sheriff Timothy Howard, Scott Patronik, Greg Savage, and Rozansky sat before the wooden railing separating the audience from the prosecutor and defendant. Steve Nigrelli and Betsy Schneider of the state police were there, as were Lissa Redmond and Amherst cops Ed Monan and Joseph LaCorte.

Dennis Delano was noticeably absent. He spent the morning with the Capozzi family.

Steven Diver and Ann Brown, Linda Yalem's sister, were escorted to the reserved section. Both felt anxiety, knowing they would be called upon to deliver a victim impact statement and recall the deaths of their loved ones in open court.

Within fifteen minutes, the carpeted gallery was filled. One surviving rape victim sat in the seventh row, anonymous in the crowd. When all the seats were occupied, people lined up against the back wall. Before the gavel pounded, it was standing room only.

At 9:23 a.m. chatter was muted as Altemio Sanchez entered from a door behind the judge's bench. Dressed in a charcoal suit, his wrists and ankles were shackled with chains. His remaining hair had been blanched gray, scruff creeping down the back of his neck. His mustache stayed black, but the goatee on his chin was lighter, trimmed tight to the flesh.

Kathleen, in the fifth row, sat up straight and craned to see over those obstructing her view. Husband and wife made no eye contact; he glanced only briefly toward the gallery and did not acknowledge that she was there. Sanchez then turned to face the judge.

Deputy district attorney Frank Sedita, middle-aged with a thick dark mustache and salt and pepper hair, made a brief statement to State Supreme Court justice Christopher Burns. The agenda was laid out: Ann Brown would speak first, with her husband by her side, then give way to Steven Diver. By prior agreement, neither would be recorded, either by audio or video.

Brown passed through the railing's hinged gate. With her back to the audience, she stepped to a podium and leaned into the microphone.

Her speech was brief but eloquent. Lasting eight minutes, she never mentioned Sanchez by name, nor did she glance to her right, where her sister's killer sat only yards away behind a wooden table.

Brown highlighted the accomplishments of Yalem's twenty-two years, recalling the timeline before she was informed that a body had been found.

"She was raped and strangled, her nose and mouth taped shut, left in the dirt with a T-shirt over her head. It is worse than your worst nightmare. How do I live with knowing what was done to my little sister? It still tortures me."

Stifling tears, Brown inhaled briefly, but continued in a composed voice. Linda had been maid of honor at her wedding. Brown's two children, born since Linda's death, are named in honor of the aunt they will never know. Tragedy had recently struck again in the Yalem family. Less than three months earlier, on May 29, Brown's mother had passed away after a long illness.

"I kept thinking about how I needed my sister with me so I didn't have to say goodbye alone," she confessed as her voice wavered. There was one positive note, however. "My mother felt relief that the killer was caught before she died."

People in the gallery shifted as Brown stepped back and gave way to Steven Diver. A thin, slight man, with blond hair spilling over the collar of his suit coat, Diver addressed the judge for more than twenty minutes, recounting Joan's life and her successes.

"Joan was my best friend," he said. "It was astonishing to see the good she could find in things." After memorializing her, he read a poem by his daughter written the previous Mother's Day. Diver admitted, "We expected to see our kids grow up and contribute to this world."

Unlike Brown, Diver did pivot to stare down his wife's killer, anger spilling from his eyes. He snarled bitterly.

"Now that I have described the warmth of Joan's soul, I want to flip everything upside down and talk about the complete antithesis: the worthless A. Sanchez. Over the past twenty years, he lied to his family and friends. He led a selfish, evil, lying life. He's deceitful, a sociopath with a complete lack of concern for anyone but himself."

On the evening of September 29, Steven and Joan planned to go to a movie. Joan's battered body was not discovered until two days later.

"Her neck looked like it had been split," Diver revealed. "After he strangled her, he beat her. We assume she was dead, but we don't know."

From the gallery, Kathleen sobbed quietly, dabbing tears with a crumpled tissue, shielding her face with a hand. Her brother touched her shoulder in consolation.

"I want you to crush any hope Sanchez has of ever leaving the walls of prison," Diver urged the judge. "He should never be able to redeem himself to a future parole board. He will lie; he's good at it. It's a mystery to me how he eluded capture all these years, because he's not a criminal mastermind."

As Diver stepped away from the microphone, his helpless anger radiated toward the opaque walls. Sanchez showed little emotion during the victim impact statements. The deputy district attorney stood, calmness replacing the other man's rage.

"There is little I can say to add light to this," Sedita admitted. "My overall impression is that he is as calculating as he is violent. He methodically selected locations, conducted reconnaissance, and practiced a double ligature technique so he could control his victims. Linda Yalem had her whole life in front of her until she ran by that guy. He made the choice to strangle her. He made the choice to duct tape her mouth. He made the choice to kill her."

Sedita paused before altering his tone. "Joan Diver wasn't raped. She was strangled to death with a wire that cost eighty cents at a hardware store."[26] In his left hand, he raised a loop of thin silver cord, displaying it for the courtroom.

"Within hours of the murder as her body lay in a field, Mr. Sanchez smiled at a party in a bar in downtown Buffalo. . . . Linda and Joan fought like hell. Majane Mazur agreed to have sexual relations with the defendant. He put a plastic bag over her head, tied a ligature, and suffocated her to death. Mazur has a nineteen-year-old daughter in South Carolina. That kid was four years old. He decided he was going to control the fate of these women.

"The recommendation of the people of New York State is that he be sent away for a minimum of twenty-five years to life for each count."

Andrew LoTempio, Sanchez's attorney, is a compact man who is respected within the legal community. Wearing a pale suit, he stood from his seat beside the defendant, asking the media to stop pestering Sanchez's family. LoTempio then told the court he had advised his client not to speak.

"Mr. Sanchez, is there anything you would like to say before sentencing?" Judge Burns asked.

LoTempio motioned for Sanchez to stand.

"Yes."

---

[26] The clerk from Hector's Hardware testified the wire cost sixty cents. Sedita quoted the price at eighty cents.

"Please keep your voice up so I can hear you."

"Yes."

In his first and only public comment, Sanchez ignored his attorney's advice to remain silent, lowering his head and leaning toward the table's microphone.

"I just wanted to mention that whatever sentence I get today, I deserve," he said softly, looking downward. "I know I'm going to be spending life behind bars, never to see the streets again. But I committed, I did these crimes, and I should pay for these crimes. To Mr. Diver and the Yalem family, I apologize, but I know I can never bring back your loved ones. But what you said today here in court is true about me. And I will pay for this for the rest of my life. Thank you."

Burns appeared unimpressed. Clad in a black robe, his face was long and thin, with a prominent nose and dark hair parted on the right. He did not idle before issuing the sentence.

"The court has the authority and the obligation to speak for this community," he said matter-of-factly. "I do not believe there is any presence of conscience here or any remorse whatsoever, except that you were caught. In the case before me, three women were slain and families hurt beyond repair. All they have now are loving memories and nightmares and none of them deserve this. You have been caught and this sentence reflects your unspeakable cruelty in committing these horrible murders. You showed no mercy and you deserve none."

As Burns read the legal charges leveled against him, Sanchez's eyes pooled for the first time. He swallowed, lower lip quivering. A tear dropped off his cheek while he clenched his lids together to clear his vision.

Sanchez was sentenced to twenty-five years to life for each of the three murders. He would spend the next seventy-five years in jail.

"It is this court's intention that you never see freedom again," Burns concluded.

With the pounding of a gavel, the Bike Path Rapist was led away and remanded to custody of state corrections officers.

It was not yet 10:30 a.m.

In the cramped basement lobby outside the courtroom, black tiled walls absorbed cones of light. LoTempio held court before TV cameras and tape recorders. Media members assembled in a tight pack opposite the elevators, corralled behind a dividing rope.

Initially, the lawyer was testy, threatening to refuse all interviews if questions continued about Sanchez's family. Task force members huddled nearby, watching the performance. They guffawed when LoTempio claimed his client had answered every question that authorities had put to him.

When LoTempio finished and stepped into the elevator, officers moved into the spotlight. Nigrelli did most of the talking, but Patronik and Sheriff Timothy Howard spoke as well. Some jockeyed for position, moving subtly behind a speaker to fall within the camera's eye.

"To solve this after only ninety days on a task force is extremely rewarding," Nigrelli admitted. "This case has been open for more than twenty years and is one of the longest open cases in the United States."

"Do you believe Sanchez is sorry?" came the question.

"No," Nigrelli replied, then considered before repeating himself more forcefully. "No, I don't. I always tell my kids, if you're going to say you're sorry, don't do it."

None of the officers, it seemed, wanted to surrender their moment of glory. Even as media began filtering away, they remained in the basement, talking among themselves, mapping out lunch plans.

It was a day to celebrate results of their hard work.

Life Sentence

Shortly after being sentenced, Altemio Sanchez was moved from the Erie County Holding Center to the Elmira Reception Center, which, in spite of its hospitable name, is another prison. He stayed there for four weeks before being transferred to Clinton Correctional Facility, located in a remote area of Northern New York nestled within the Adirondack Mountains. Here he was assigned to the Assessment and Program Preparation Unit, nicknamed "APP," reserved for high-profile prisoners who might be targeted by fellow inmates if left to mingle in the general population.

Although he had never been in jail before, Sanchez spent all but the first fifteen days of 2007 locked up. As the year progressed, grim reality dawned that this mundane pattern, this dull drone of days, would encompass the remainder of his life.

At Clinton, Sanchez fell into an awkward routine. Most of the time he was confined to his cell, but six times per week he was allowed into the yard during two-hour blocks. He took advantage of the opportunity to leave the cell, shooting baskets or lifting weights to rehabilitate an old shoulder injury. There was even talk of getting a prison job. Being fluent in Spanish, he was asked to assist in bilingual education. He was intrigued by the idea, but because he was incarcerated for life, Sanchez would have to wait until there was an opening. Inmates with a scheduled release date were given priority on such work.

Some fellow prisoners from Western New York recognized his name and therefore knew he was the Bike Path Rapist. Sanchez kept to himself, hoping to avoid trouble. A fellow inmate had attacked him in the Erie County Holding Center, but during his first few months, there were no problems in his new jail.

Visits from his family stopped. His oldest son lived outside San Diego, and had traveled to Elmira during a return trip to Western New York. His wife remained an ally before his confession. Since the sentencing, he still spoke with Kathleen, but for the most part, he felt alone. Part of the reason was Sanchez's admission of guilt. Another was that Clinton was a long way from Buffalo.

That fall, Kathleen filed for divorce, which was granted in October. Sanchez knew it was coming and understood why, but the end of his marriage remained devastating. Perhaps more than being arrested, the split signaled a break with his past life. Kathleen had been his first and only girlfriend, allowing him to overcome his shyness. When he was around her, he was never consumed by dark feelings of fantasy and anger. Her presence in his life may have kept him from even more trouble.

During long blocks of quiet time, he often reflected on the disconnect that ruled his life. On the one hand he was a family man, married for twenty-six years with two grown boys. He worked his job on the night shift and played golf and softball. He had coached Little League and took pride in his sons. He owned a house in the suburbs and earned the respect of his neighbors. By all appearances, he led a worthwhile existence.

But there was another side of him, a side that no one had known. How had he become a serial rapist and killer? Was that really even him? Until his capture, his closest contacts had no inkling of his dark side—not his wife, nor his children. He had confided in no one, although Sanchez wondered if Uncle Freddie suspected his buried secrets. But his existence as a rapist and killer was so opposed to everything that he represented.

If only he could explain it to someone. If only he understood it himself. As a teen, he experienced blackouts. Later, the pressure built into a vortex of rage. When those spells came on, the only thing that would quell them was to take control of a woman. He knew it was wrong. They were innocent victims. But he had to seize someone, fulfill his fantasy, and release the pent-up urge. It was the only way to feel better.

In a conversation after his confession, Kathleen told him that he should have confided to her about his desires. She would have insisted he undergo counseling.

"I was afraid to say anything to my wife because of the fear of her leaving me," he said. "And I know she was right. I should have got help, but I didn't. I just kept on doing these crimes."

His dark side spiraled out of control. He predicted it would happen and foresaw the endgame. Eventually, the truth caught up to him.

*

On Thursday, November 8, 2007, nearly three months after sentencing, Sanchez woke early and donned an olive green turtleneck with a white nametag stitched to the breast. Sliding into a matching pullover, Sanchez was informed he was being taken off prison grounds for the day, but was not told why. He had only been at Clinton for a short time, but even he knew this was a break in protocol.

At first he thought of his shoulder injury. He was being shuttled to a doctor for X-rays, he speculated, maybe some physical therapy. Upon his arrest ten months earlier, a jailhouse examination revealed high blood pressure. Perhaps that had nudged higher, and he needed immediate treatment.

He was shackled around his waist, and additional chains and cuffs bound his wrists and feet. His gait was relegated to tentative baby steps. Likewise, his hands could not stray far from their position near his stomach.

Placed in the backseat of a secured car, he was driven from the facility. It was a gray dawn, and the surrounding roads and trees were unfamiliar. He considered that he should revel in the scenery and appreciate the autumn air, because such sights would be rare throughout his remaining years.

The reason for his day trip had nothing to do with his health. A team of officers, several from the disbanded task force, had traveled more than six hours to Lake Placid for another interview. There were still unanswered questions. How many rapes had Sanchez done? Had he ever murdered anyone else? Were there times he was close to being caught? How intricate were his plans? Who knew what he was doing? What really happened to Joan Diver on that fateful morning?

His sentence would not be lengthened. He was already incarcerated for life. Facing that reality, the hope was that he would finally come clean.

The previous day, Scott Patronik drove from Buffalo with Greg Savage, Alan Rozansky, and Dennis Delano. Josh Keats and Betsy Schneider from the state police arrived separately, along with Tonawanda detective Brian Moline, who wanted to ask about the unsolved murder of a teenage girl in his town. Two profilers from the FBI were on hand, planning to participate in the interview as well.

"That night, we all met up at a bar and Josh and Betsy were having beers with the feds when we arrived," Delano recalled. "Because he felt there was a rapport with Sanchez on the day of the arrest, Josh convinced them that he could have done more in a different situation."

Although they did not secure a confession during Sanchez's initial interview the previous January, observers believed that Keats and Lissa Redmond—the last team to interrogate him during the marathon nine-and-a-half-hour interview—had come closest to reaching the truth. An unusual incident two days later fueled the intrigue. While in a high-security cell at the Erie County Holding Center, Sanchez informed guards that he wanted to speak to Keats and Redmond again. The detectives were contacted at their Oak Street offices, but by the time they reached the jail, Sanchez had changed his mind.

"The profilers thought there might be some connection there, so they believed Keats should talk to Sanchez," Savage said. "But Lissa was sick and couldn't come with us."

Federal agents determined Keats would do the initial questioning before giving way to others. The decision did not sit well with cops from other jurisdictions. State police had not been the primary investigators on any of the rapes or murders, so why should they get first crack at asking questions?

"It was the Feds' call to send Keats in," Delano noted. "That decision was made at the top."

That morning, officers rendezvoused at a state police barracks several miles from Clinton Correctional Facility. Sanchez was ushered into a small room with a table and chairs. Blinds were drawn over an outside window. A one-way mirror concealed a video camera set up to record the proceedings.

Those not in the interview area watched a closed-circuit TV feed from a locker room down the hall. It was next to a gym, where the noise of clanking weights sometimes drowned out the serial killer's words.

"It wasn't the best situation," Delano noted. "We had to ask a guy to turn off his treadmill so we could hear."

Keats, clad in a dress shirt and tie, entered the room and re-introduced himself to Sanchez. The prisoner still had no idea why he was there.

"You remember me at all?" Keats asked, thrusting a palm toward the restrictive chains on the prisoner's lap.

"Yes . . . yes I do," Sanchez replied, shaking hands awkwardly, bewilderment fading from his face as he gazed up toward the standing investigator. "You talked to me . . . I think with Lissa."

Keats professed he was there to gather information that would help him become a better investigator. Perhaps Sanchez had insights or additional details that would help put to rest some of the lingering questions authorities had. It was short notice, but would Sanchez be willing to talk?

He considered for a moment. Maybe he realized that if he refused, he would be shuttled back to the APP Unit, spending the rest of his day mired in monotony. Maybe he agreed to sit through another interview to discover how much the cops really knew. Or maybe he thought that he could toy with authorities one more time. Whatever the motive, he agreed to answer questions. It was clear he wanted to see Lissa Redmond again. He inquired about her twice during the next seven hours, even asking if she observed the proceedings from behind the one-way mirror to his left.

"When Lissa questioned him on the day he was arrested, he accused her of trying to get into his head," Delano recalled. "He thought she was a psychiatrist and didn't believe she was a cop. Something about her spooked him pretty good."

"There's no question the guy has problems with women," Savage added. "Her not being there changed the dynamics of that interview."

Keats spent the next three hours talking to Sanchez about a wide array of topics. They spoke of his childhood, meeting his wife, and growing up on Buffalo's west side.[27] Like Sanchez, Keats had played baseball in school, and Sanchez mentioned he was proud of his sons' athletic achievements. One had recently bowled a 299.

More often, however, the conversation centered on crimes committed. Sanchez contradicted himself several times and was foggy about dates, times, and rapes that occurred. He could not even recall what year he graduated from high school.

Before sentencing, Sanchez had reviewed cases with the district attorney's office. With his lawyer, both parties determined that he had attacked between eleven and fourteen women. This is roughly half the number for which the task force believes Sanchez was responsible.

"It couldn't be higher," Sanchez insisted. "I had all these when I spoke to the DA. We went through every rape case he could think of. One had to do with a woman who was attacked when she was working on a house. That wasn't me. I wouldn't approach a woman in a residential area. I went to secluded places. In the beginning I thought it was seven or eight, but we came to eleven. I know the crimes I committed. I have nothing to hide. I'm locked up for life, so why shouldn't I tell you?"

---

[27] In this interview, Sanchez asserted that his mother's boyfriend abused him while he was a boy and the trauma has lasted his entire life.

"We did research but could find no indication that occurred," Delano noted. "All we learned was that mom caught dad in bed with a hooker while they were still in Puerto Rico. There was no evidence of anything else. I think Sanchez said that because after his arrest, news people called psychologists for a quote, and they suggested he may have been abused as a kid. People are always looking for a reason to blame somebody instead of taking responsibility for their actions."

His next words, however, were telling.

"So far, we've ended up with eleven," he said.

Observers watching the interview scribbled furiously, noting how he adhered to a number after slipping in a subtle qualifier.

He remembered his attacks based on location and clothing that the victim wore. He had never raped or killed anyone out of state, in spite of vacations to the western United States and Europe. But even that declaration might have been tinged with untruth.

"I can pinpoint exactly every location where these rapes happened," Sanchez told Keats. "I don't remember names of streets, but I know where. I've never done a crime while on a trip. The only crimes I've ever committed were in the Buffalo area. Here I had the rope and tape. We went on vacations to a lot of different places, but it never crossed my mind to do anything outside of the Buffalo area."

After talking about visits to Las Vegas and San Diego, he added, "Any crimes that I've committed are mostly in the Buffalo area."

Keats pounced on the inconsistency. "Mostly? Please don't lie to me. It's not going to have any affect on the amount of time you serve."

"I'm in jail anyways," Sanchez agreed. "What do I have to hide?"

After insisting he had told the district attorney everything he knew, he admitted to two additional rapes that he had not mentioned before. One occurred near Bidwell Parkway; the other happened along the Niagara Section of the New York State Thruway between Elmwood and Grant Streets, near Scajaquada Creek.

He estimated he was nineteen or twenty years old during the first attack. He was living with his mother at the time. He approached a girl on a bike and bashed her in the head. While she was stunned, he waved a knife and ordered her to remove her pants while he did the same. He claims he did not penetrate the victim, but only rubbed against her.

"I didn't knock her out or anything," he said. "I had a box cutter. I told her to shut up and take her pants down. I just laid on top of her, got my sexual fantasy, and that was it. It wasn't to a point where I inserted my penis in her. I didn't go that far. I was too scared."

In the second attack, he spotted a woman walking alone. The area was deserted, so he grabbed her hair and pulled her off the road. Cars passed as he accosted her just out of sight.

"I told her 'Don't say anything or you're going to get hurt.' But I didn't hurt her. I just laid on top of her and had my sexual fantasy. I couldn't control it."

Keats wondered if Sanchez needed more water or if he wanted to remove his pullover. Sanchez was fine, but Keats excused himself for the lavatory. Once out of the room, he requested details about past cases from the observing detectives.

"Josh didn't have enough information to question him intelligently," Delano said. "Sanchez lied because he could and Josh didn't know enough to call him on it. Josh wanted specifics from us, then went back to the interview trying to get more. By the afternoon, after they had been talking for a couple hours, there was no progress being made. Sanchez was cooperative, but he wasn't giving us anything."

Sanchez did know that another man had been indicted for two rapes he had committed. He claimed, however, that he did not learn of this until years later.[28]

Sanchez had been promised any lunch he wanted. He requested a hamburger, complaining that prison food was high in carbohydrates and generally unhealthy; he had lost forty pounds after his arrest because of his changing diet. The menu order fell on deaf ears, however. After 12:30 p.m., pizza, chicken wings, and cola were brought in.

Keats asked if Sanchez would be willing to talk to additional investigators. He agreed, and during the next several hours, a parade of officers funneled in and out of the room. For sixty minutes, an FBI profiler tried to pinpoint the differences between anger and fantasy, asking Sanchez to elaborate on conflicting emotions and triggers that fueled his rage. Later Savage took a turn, trying to clarify details of Joan Diver's murder.

Sanchez remained puzzled that forensics asserted the weapon used to murder Joan Diver was a loop of wire. He denied ever using a cable, saying it would be impractical. Unlike rope, wire was not flexible and would not fold easily into his pocket. He insisted that he always used a homemade ligature with rope and broom handles. After a rape, he sliced the nylon cord into pieces and dumped it

---

[28] Ironically, Anthony Capozzi's sister, Pam Guenther, attended Grover Cleveland High School at the same time as Sanchez. "After I looked through old yearbooks, I remembered him vaguely," Guenther said. "He always had a very scary look. He was not somebody you wanted to have direct contact with."

in a public trash can. He claimed the rope used on Diver was discarded in a wastebasket at the Galleria Mall.

None of the investigators can explain why Sanchez adamantly denies using a wire.

"I think he's lying," Delano theorized. "But I can't tell you why. Who can say why he would lie about any of that stuff?"

"We matched that cable with the imprints on Joan Diver's neck," Rozansky explained. "We also had someone testify that she sold a piece of wire to that particular guy. I can't imagine a lady subjecting herself to perjury over that if it wasn't true. But you don't always know what's the truth or a lie with him."

When Savage left, another officer came in to question Sanchez, and talk turned to the unsolved homicide of teenager Katherine Herold along railroad tracks in Kenmore from 1985.

"I didn't have anything to do with that crime," Sanchez said. "I'll be glad to take a lie detector test. The only three victims are the ones I've been charged with. I've never murdered anybody else."

Nearing 4:00 p.m., Sanchez had been seated in a small room for nearly seven hours. In that time, he stood only briefly, to have his restraints loosened so he could feed himself and to point out locations on a map spread across the table. During a break, he sighed, and said to the guard, "A lot of questions."

Answers, however, were in short supply.

"It was very obvious he would talk to anybody," Savage reflected after spending an hour face to face with the killer that day. "It didn't matter who it was. You could send Bozo the clown in there. Most of what he was saying was bullshit anyway.

"Maybe his recollection wasn't clear, but during that interview every question that we put to him he was thinking and he lied more often than not. He had contradictory answers to the same questions asked at separate times. He doesn't have a great memory for dates, but I also believe he was calculating."

One of the last things Sanchez said was that he was willing to assist more in the future.

"When you commit crimes as much as I did, you're going to remember what happened," Sanchez reflected. "If somebody asks me about a certain area, I'll fill you in. To be honest with you, I don't mind what's going on here. It's good to be out. You guys got me pretty good. I gave you everything I could."

After a long day spent monitoring the proceedings, Patronik had mixed emotions about the interview's effectiveness.

"We had to do it, because we would always wonder if we could have gotten more information from him. Overall, I didn't get a good feel. For certain things Sanchez would tell the truth and for other things he'd lie. The stuff we can't prove, I don't know how much of it was true."

Delano remains upset that more was not accomplished during the jailhouse interview.

"It wasn't handled right by the Feds or the state police," he said. "Sanchez only gave us what we already knew. I was ticked off about taking a backseat to every-one else. I didn't get the chance to talk to Sanchez and that burned me. I had my notes and know I could have confronted him on the lies."

Why weren't Delano's skills as a homicide investiga-tor called into play? He is an experienced interrogator who understood the specifics of rape and murder cases. He believes politics influenced who was allowed to par-ticipate in the interview.

"I'm not taking anything away from the guys who talked to Sanchez, but in the city we get so many homi-cides that you start to get good at investigations, even if it's just by accident," he noted. "Some people had the atti-tude that we should talk to Sanchez about anything, then next time we come for a follow-up interview, he'll be our friend. Bullshit. We needed facts, but it wasn't handled the right way."

As time passes, no new revelations are expected. Women of Western New York are no longer potential victims of this serial rapist. With the murderer locked away, the case is closed.

Even though it would not change the outcome, Del-ano would like the chance to talk with Sanchez. If he was assured of a one-on-one interview, he believes he could get the killer to open up.

"Right now there hasn't been a long enough period for him to sit without anybody messing with him," the detective mused. "Cops from other jurisdictions go there trying to connect him to unsolved cases. Reporters are still trying to interview him, but he won't talk. After some time in his cell without all these distractions, he might feel differently."

Delano's Last Case

For Delano, lightning struck twice in the same year. The Bike Path Rapist was the first of two high-profile cold cases in which he discovered that an innocent person was jailed. While the release of Anthony Capozzi brought Delano to the media's attention in early 2007, the next series of cases—culminating with the 1993 murder of thirteen-year-old Crystallynn Girard—thrust him into the limelight and effectively ended his police career.

A fellow parishioner at his church, Trish Radzikowski, approached Delano. Because of publicity from the Bike Path investigation, she knew he was a cold case expert and wondered if he would revisit her sister's unsolved murder fourteen years earlier.

"No promises, but I'll take a look," he told her.

Delano pulled the files and began reading. He learned that on September 9, 1993, forty-two-year-old Joan Giambra was strangled and left nude in her Buffalo home. Suspicion immediately fell toward her estranged husband, Sam. The couple had been planning to divorce. But skin samples taken from beneath Joan's fingernails suggested a struggle with her killer. That DNA did not match with Sam Giambra, who committed suicide in 2000.

Delano and fellow cold case investigators were intrigued. They began accumulating DNA swabs from anyone related to the case. One of Giambra's daughters recalled a man who contacted her shortly after her mother's murder, a bartender named Dennis. He claimed to have dated Joan and wondered if there was any progress in tracking her killer.

The bartender's full name was Dennis Donahue. By 2007, he was unemployed and living with relatives in Western New York. Lissa Redmond, by then a cold case detective, approached him to submit a DNA swab. Donahue agreed.

It was a mistake that cost him a life in prison.

His sample matched the skin cells found beneath Joan Giambra's fingernails. Detectives quickly built a case against him. After fourteen years of delayed justice, another long-standing unsolved murder was put to rest.[29]

But Delano noticed similarities to two other homicides whose files he had read. One occurred on September 9, 1975, eighteen years to the day before the Giambra killing. A middle-aged woman, Carol Reed, was found naked and strangled in her Buffalo apartment. Donahue lived down the hall and had been considered a person of interest before the case fizzled.

On Valentine's Day in 1993, thirteen-year-old Crystallynn Girard was found dead in the bedroom of her South Buffalo home, nude and strangled. Her mother, Lynn DeJac, had been convicted of that murder and was

---

[29] Donahue, fifty-five, was found guilty for this murder in May 2008.

serving twenty-five years to life in jail. While it was not unusual for a prisoner to claim innocence, as DeJac did, suspicion was raised when it was learned that she dated Donahue and the two had a bitter and public fight on the night of Crystallynn's death.

"If you looked at the three murders, they were very similar," Delano noted. "Two were on Donahue's birthday, which is September 9. All the victims were nude, found lying face up, and he was acquainted with each of them. There were just too many similarities to overlook."

In an ironic twist, Andrew LoTempio, the lawyer who defended Sanchez, had also served as DeJac's attorney more than a decade earlier. Losing that trial had always bothered him. He wholeheartedly believed in DeJac's innocence.

Delano phoned the lawyer for background information.

"She didn't do it," was the first thing LoTempio said.

Facts from that case painted a bleak picture. In 1993, DeJac was a twenty-nine-year-old single mother who worked at the family bar a few doors away from her South Buffalo home. On Valentine's Day night, she attended a wedding with Donahue, whom she had been dating. When they returned to her house, nearing midnight, she told him their relationship was over and an argument ensued. As threats escalated, DeJac phoned police, but Donahue slapped the receiver from her hand. Crystallynn completed the call from another room. Donahue stormed away in a rage, and DeJac ventured to the bar. On her way out, she cautioned her daughter not to answer the door lest police accuse her of child abandonment.

Shortly after that, Donahue entered the tavern. He watched as DeJac flirted with an old boyfriend. Donahue's blood boiled as DeJac went out the door with the other man. At 4:30 that morning, DeJac and her friend ventured back to her home to check on Crystallynn. The girl was asleep in bed.

DeJac—either unconcerned or unaware that Donahue was stalking her in a rage—left again to spend the night with the man from the bar. Returning home at noon the next day, she discovered Crystallynn lying on her bed, wearing nothing but a pair of red socks. The girl was not breathing. Her face was bruised and a puncture wound penetrated her chest.

Police interviewed DeJac and Donahue separately. Donahue passed a polygraph test in which he admitted using cocaine that night but claimed to have no knowledge of Crystallynn's death. As police built a case against the grieving mother, Donahue testified against DeJac before a grand jury.

The most damning implication that DeJac murdered her daughter came from an informant. He was an acquaintance who claimed that after Crystallynn's death, DeJac sat on a barstool and admitted to the killing. The accuser, Wayne Hudson, was a twice-convicted felon who was facing a third strike and a possible long-term prison stint. Although no one can prove he traded information for a lighter sentence, his charge was reduced to a misdemeanor and he avoided jail.

At trial, DeJac denied any involvement. But that was not enough. Many believe her conviction was based more on a questionable lifestyle than the facts surrounding the case.

"I didn't do this," she insisted, tears spilling from her eyes. The judge sentenced her to twenty-five years to life.

"Nothing about that trial added up," Delano lamented, shaking his head. "The timeline from that night only gave her fifteen minutes to kill her daughter. There were so many things that didn't make sense."

In 2007, cold case detectives visited DeJac in jail. They also submitted blood from the crime scene for retesting.

District attorney Frank Clark was not pleased. He had been an assistant DA during the first trial in 1994. *Dateline NBC* claimed that Clark was a key player in the decision to allow Donahue's testimony at the grand jury, an act that automatically granted him immunity from prosecution. Therefore, even if investigators proved that Donahue was responsible for Crystallynn's murder, he could not be tried.

Although Delano does not know from where the order originated, he and his colleagues were instructed by the chief of detectives to relax the investigation.

Delano would do no such thing.

Lab results came back just as they anticipated: Donahue's DNA was found in and around Crystallynn's body. With enough reasonable doubt, in November 2007, a judge ordered Lynn DeJac released from prison.

The district attorney was furious, immediately vowing to conduct a new trial for DeJac.

"Never in a million, billion years would we not retry this," Clark stated boldly to TV cameras.

On the heels of Anthony Capozzi's release, Lynn DeJac's wrongful imprisonment was the DA's second public relations nightmare inside a year. Clark went on the offensive, claiming that Donahue's DNA at the scene did not prove he killed Crystallynn. He implied that the forty-one-year-old man might have been having consensual sex with a thirteen-year-old girl.

"I think what he said is sick and twisted," Delano said.

While Delano was ordered off the case, Clark hired a new medical examiner to review the original autopsy reports. In 1993, Dr. Sung-ook Baik, then the associate chief Erie County medical examiner, determined Crystallynn died of manual strangulation. Clark sought the second opinion of Dr. Michael Baden, a pathologist for hire who had worked on O. J. Simpson's trial. He reached an entirely different conclusion.[30]

Crystallynn Girard was not strangled to death. Instead, Baden insisted, she succumbed to a cocaine overdose. Dr. James Woytash, Erie County's current medical examiner, agreed.

"We no longer have a criminal case," Clark declared on February 13, 2008. DeJac was free without stipulation and there would be no retrial.

Those close to the investigation were outraged. Crystallynn had been an honor student. She was not a drug user, nor was she having an affair with her mother's boyfriend. According to Delano, the amount of cocaine

---

[30] Due to some far-fetched theories Baden had reached in other cases such as O.J. Simpson and the shooting of actress Lana Clarkson, a newspaper columnist suggested his business card should read "Conclusions to Suit Your Needs."

in her system was so small that it would barely have an effect on her. His explanation for the drug's presence was that Donahue violated her, with powder residue on his fingers.

Pathologists debated the new findings. One of the key reasons that strangulation was eliminated from the updated exam is because the hyoid bone in Crystallynn's neck was not broken. But experts argued that the bone might remain intact if she was choked because the hyoid is still flexible in a teenager's body.

Others claimed that trace amounts of cocaine were misleading because the drug metabolized into benzoylecgonine. There was a higher percentage of that in her system, according to toxicology reports.

The only thing everyone agreed on was that there was no clear-cut answer to how the girl died. But it raised many ethical questions surrounding the district attorney's behavior.

Was this a convenient escape alley? By ruling the death an overdose, there would be no criminal charges and more importantly, no trial. The DA's office could not be accused of bungling the case years ago by granting immunity to a suspected killer.

After this bombshell, Delano fumed at the injustice. He believed people were manipulating facts and smearing the memory of a thirteen-year-old to avoid facing responsibility. He took a day off from work and flew to Washington, D.C., where he sought the opinion of forensic experts. Accompanying him was Scott Brown, a reporter from WGRZ-TV. Delano supplied that news station with a copy of the 1993 crime scene video from

Crystallynn's room, revealing overturned furniture and blood-stained walls. There was clear evidence of a struggle. The overdose theory did not address the chaos around the bed, her bruised face, or cuts on her chest.

Delano's dogged pursuit of truth continued to bother his superiors. He had been ordered off the case yet refused to comply.

On February 27, Delano was suspended without pay for releasing evidence to the media. His gun and shield were confiscated and he was escorted from headquarters. Buffalo police commissioner H. McCarthy Gibson claimed Delano "broke the chain of command."

Delano, however, believed he did no such thing. He admitted providing the tape of Crystallynn's bedroom to the media, but argued there was no harm in that because no case existed.

"The district attorney said there was no crime committed because Crystallynn died of a cocaine overdose," he said. "If there is no crime, how can there be evidence?"

For several weeks, the dual stories of Crystallynn's mysterious death and Delano's suspension dominated the news cycle in Western New York. Friends from the Bike Path Rapist task force organized a benefit for Delano at a downtown bar on a chilly Sunday in March. More than five hundred people attended, paying twenty dollars at the door for food, drinks, and a chance to meet the detective. Most of those in attendance were strangers to Delano.

"I can't believe the support I've had," he reflected. "Everywhere I go, people stop me and say thanks. These are people of every race from all different walks of life. I can't stroll through a grocery store without being recognized. It's a bit embarrassing."

Endorsement was not unanimous, however. A handful of officers spoke out against Delano's choice to release the videotape to the media. One retired cop who worked the original homicide in 1993 remained convinced that DeJac was the killer and publicly criticized Delano's actions.

Frank Clark declared he had no involvement with Delano's suspension, and the police commissioner seconded that, saying the decision was his alone.

On March 29, 2008, Delano's pay was reinstated after thirty days. But for the next several months he remained off duty, suspended until a hearing was scheduled.

"I'm waiting for my day in court," Delano mused as spring turned to summer and no date had been set. "I was embarrassed by the way they treated me. My stuff is still in my desk and I can't go back there. Just before this happened, I was bypassed for a promotion, but I haven't been convicted of anything. This is not how our justice system should work, but higher-ups are playing games with me."

Meanwhile, Crystallynn Girard's cause of death officially remains a cocaine overdose. While that bothers many, no effort is underway to re-examine the case.

Delano's public struggle has proved to be both a curse and a blessing. His police career is likely over. If his suspension is lifted and he is called back to work, he plans to retire immediately, because he has lost faith in the bosses he worked for. The motivation for investigating cold cases was to seek the truth and reveal long-standing injustices. He was a tenacious worker who molded himself into an expert. Delano is pleased there are several other cold case officers who continue this important work. His forced exit, however, deprives the community of Delano's accumulated knowledge and expertise. He misses the job.

On the other hand, because of his high profile, he now has a wider platform to battle public offenses. His discovery of two people wrongfully imprisoned has led him to wonder how many more are facing a similar fate.

Delano's visibility brought him unexpected opportunities as well. After being approached by the Republican Party, he agreed to run for the New York State Senate. Delano announced his candidacy in May, with members of the Capozzi and DeJac families by his side.

Asked by a reporter if he was trying to capitalize on his fame, Delano proved that even in the realm of politics, he would remain unpretentious and straightforward.

"You're absolutely right," he admitted. "Otherwise, why do you think someone would make me an offer to run for office?"

He made no campaign promises other than to investigate what happens to the tax money that citizens of Western New York send to the state capital in Albany. The election, in November 2008, pitted Delano against a longtime Democratic incumbent in a district with three times as many registered Democrats. Delano briefly led in the polls, but was narrowly defeated after an aggressive media blitz by his opponent.

Delano never envisioned himself seeking political office, but then again, as a young man, he did not aspire to be a cop.

Being involved with the Bike Path case has changed his life indelibly. The irony is that after becoming a recognized name in Western New York for his tenacity and willingness to confront the system, he has been suspended for pursuing the truth—the very reason the Cold Case Squad was created.

"In retrospect, it killed one aspect of his career, but he's managed to turn that into a positive by launching a different one," Savage reflected.

Afterword: Effects

There are unusual facets to the Bike Path Rapist case, and many questions remain. The behavior of Altemio Sanchez does not always match expectations, based on what experts know about serial rapists and killers.

It remains baffling how an average man draped in the appearance of a normal life led a double existence. How is it that no one from his family or work knew his dark secrets? After dozens of attacks in different locations, how did he elude capture for so long?

How could the wrong man spend twenty-two years behind bars for crimes he did not commit? What does it say about the American justice system that Anthony Capozzi was convicted based on circumstantial evidence but was not eligible for release until scientific proof was discovered?

While this case is unique, it does contain similarities to other killers who have led double lives. Dennis Rader, infamously known as BTK, was active in a Lutheran church in Wichita, Kansas. As a Cub Scout leader and longtime city employee, he was the picture of stability. Gary Ridgeway, the Green River killer who preyed on prostitutes in the Pacific Northwest, was married, raised a son, and attended church regularly. He held the same job for thirty-two years.

Yet in spite of the parallels, for many reasons, Alte-mio Sanchez remains an enigma. Most people keep some secrets, even from those closest to them. But few rape and murder over a period spanning nearly three decades.

After spending an extensive amount of time with him, lawyer Andrew LoTempio suggested that Sanchez is mentally ill, but has never been diagnosed. Is Sanchez a conniving liar or one who truly does not understand parameters that surround him? He displays elements of both. He often misstates simple things, perhaps con-vincing himself that they are true. He does not seem to understand cause and effect or chronology.

Delano refers to "the disconnect" that permeated the killer's life. When normal behavior came into conflict with his desires, he was able to separate and compart-mentalize, allowing both to co-exist.

"We listened to Sanchez explain himself," Delano said. "I got the impression he had this steady urge that burned inside. But he didn't consciously act on it. He had a desire, then found himself in a position to satisfy it. I don't think when he woke up that day he believed he would commit rape. Somewhere in his mind, he knew it was going to happen, but the normal part of him didn't want to accept it. He tried to suppress that urge. Then he found himself on a bike path wandering around the woods, saw somebody jogging by, felt the ligature in his pocket, and realized, *There's my opportunity.* When it was over, part of him thought, *Holy shit, I did it again.*"

There are several elements of the case that break from the existing knowledge on serial killers. Although it is not unprecedented, it is unusual that for twelve years, between a rape in 1994 and Joan Diver's homicide in 2006, he apparently ceased his violent behavior.[31] Most serial murderers are empowered by each undetected attack. Success fuels desire. The longer they elude capture, the more emboldened their actions become. They often begin to taunt authorities.

Sanchez was just the opposite.

"I was scared to get caught because of the murders," he admitted. "Very, very scared. I had a talk with myself and stopped for many years. I knew if I started again, I would be caught."

Delano admits this is difficult to understand, but finds credence in the explanation.

"As twisted as it sounds, why else would he suppress this for twelve years?" the detective mused. "I think part of him wanted to stop, but it was his nature to continue.

"Still, he kept himself in situations where he could rape. All of a sudden, he found himself in the middle of it. Afterward, he acted normally. He probably even put it out of his head, telling himself, *I don't think I really did that.* That's why he was able to pull it off without anyone suspecting him.

"If he planned too much, he probably would have been caught. When criminals act on the spur of the moment, often they won't be captured. They didn't know what they were going to do ahead of time, so when you investigate, things don't fit into a neat pattern. It's tough

---

[31] While some investigators theorize that he probably did conduct attacks during this time, as yet no crimes can be linked to him through forensics.

to trace because they're improvising rather than following a plan."

Although Sanchez did not conduct any attacks near his Cheektowaga home, a rape happened one-fifth of a mile from American Brass. Other rapes occurred only blocks from his former residence on Inwood Place, beside Delaware Park in Buffalo. This is unusual because serial killers often leave a buffer zone around their house and place of employment.

"This case does not fit a geographic profile," Delano explained. "Sanchez committed rapes on railroad tracks that ran right past his workplace. Victims could see the factory's smokestacks."

Perhaps the most intriguing mystery, however, is whether Sanchez ever took "souvenirs" from the girls he assaulted. According to research, a serial rapist often keeps a trinket from a victim to remind himself of the attack. By looking at it later, the rapist can recall details of his conquest and relive the excitement of those moments. The keepsake becomes a valued talisman.

"You can't tell me that he didn't keep a record somewhere," Delano insisted. "Some women realized they were missing items that were never found at the crime scene. For instance, we never located Joan Diver's hat. Where did it go? A baseball hat doesn't just disappear. In another case, a woman lost a piece of jewelry."

Thus far, no one has been able to prove that Sanchez took anything to remember his victims. He claims he never did. Authorities searched Sanchez's home and workplace, but no traces of souvenirs were found. Delano remains undeterred.

"He's got those things hidden," Delano believes. "I don't see how he could have destroyed them before we arrested him. It's probably stashed in a secret compartment in his house or his garage, some very secure place where his wife wouldn't have found it."

Another element that has never been resolved is the mysterious newspaper article that arrived at police headquarters three days before Joan Diver's murder. The name "Arnold Ware" was printed on the paper's back.

Because Sanchez was captured, most investigators have deemed the clue irrelevant, a fluke in a case littered with too many complexities. But Delano would like to see that loose end brought to a conclusion.

"Everybody forgot about this," he said. "I'd like that letter to be sent to the Feds in Quantico, where they have top-notch document examiners. Maybe then we'd get some answers."

In interviews after his arrest, Sanchez denied having any involvement with mailing the photocopy, and Delano believes him. It simply doesn't fit his m.o. Unlike some serial killers, he did not like to draw attention to himself.

"It doesn't appear that Sanchez and Ware knew each other," the detective said. "My initial thought was that if Sanchez was aware Capozzi was mentally unstable and had taken the fall for rapes he didn't commit, maybe Sanchez tried to set up another guy for a murder he was going to do. Did he know that Ware was a screwball and somehow try to get him implicated? But unlike Capozzi, Ware doesn't look anything like Sanchez. That is such a long shot that it's almost implausible. The whole thing about that letter makes no sense whatsoever."

In spite of the impressive accomplishments of the task force, some questions may never be answered.

Because of the case's high profile, involvement with the Bike Path Rapist has been life changing for many of the key players who investigated and prosecuted the crimes.

A few months after Sanchez's capture, Lissa Redmond left Buffalo's Sex Crimes Unit and joined Delano in the Cold Case Squad. The two became close friends. For nearly a year, the veteran mentored the younger officer in techniques and methods for solving crimes.

"Dennis and I are an odd pair," Redmond said. "I joked that I was Dr. Watson to his Sherlock Holmes. In a way, it felt like I was working with my father. That's the type of relationship we had."

When Anthony Capozzi was released, Delano and Redmond were in the courtroom as the judge read the order. Overcome by emotion, TV cameras filmed them hugging afterward. When Redmond met the Capozzi family later, they recognized her, but mistook her for Delano's daughter.

With Delano gone from the office, Redmond continues in the Cold Case Squad, working on behalf of victims neglected by time.

Because of his efforts with the task force, Sheriff Alan Rozansky saw his title change from detective to senior detective. He remains proud of his contribution to the team's effort.

"This is the biggest case of my career," he reflected. "I've busted well-known drug dealers and other criminals.

But to arrest somebody for serial murders and rapes and at the same time discover an innocent man who is freed as a result of it, that's where this story is more than just the average copper case."

Rozansky sees the experience as a reminder about the importance of good police work. Often, his job entails sending bad guys to jail. In this case, he also sought freedom for an incarcerated man. Although the process was grueling, the result was satisfying beyond words.

On Tuesday, April 3, 2007, Rozansky traveled to the Buffalo Psychiatric Center to check on Capozzi, who had spent decades in prison before being released earlier that day.

"I . . . I . . . I remember you," Capozzi said upon seeing the detective. "You came to visit me in Attica."

Their meeting in December was the catalyst that convinced authorities of Capozzi's innocence. Now free, Capozzi fished into his pocket and withdrew a piece of red-colored hard candy twisted in clear plastic.

"T . . . T . . . This is for you," Capozzi offered.

Rozansky's eyes grow cloudy as he recounts the story.

"This guy is locked up for twenty-two years for something he didn't do, and he's bringing me candy?"

It was a moment the veteran lawman will always cherish. Now wrapped in a protective layer of aluminum foil, Rozansky still carries the candy in his pocket everywhere he goes. He calls it "a good luck charm" and it serves as a reminder of the best his job has to offer.

Sheriff Greg Savage was promoted from sergeant to lieutenant at the end of 2007, but the bump was not directly linked to his success with the task force.

"I was next on the civil service list," he said with a smile. Although he continues to do the same type of work, experience in hunting the serial rapist has taught him lessons about human nature.

"There are people out there with dark secrets, and they mask them very well," he reflected. "The case was part of local history, certainly the biggest one I've ever been involved in."

After twenty-seven years with the Amherst Police Department, Detective Ed Monan retired in September 2007. Since the early 1980s, he had watched colleagues pursue the Bike Path case, often following leads that screeched into dead ends. Sanchez's capture was the capstone to his career.

"It may be the biggest case that's happened in Western New York," he mused. "You're talking about a triple homicide that has been open forever."

Monan understands why criticism has been lobbed at his agency. Before Monan was assigned the file, Amherst had Sanchez in its sights in the early 1990s, conducting surveillance on his home and interviewing him at the station. But he disagrees that his department missed any obvious signs.

"We're very thorough," he said. "The fact that we interviewed him isn't unique. We interview everybody. If a neighbor calls in something about a person, we interview him. Sanchez came in voluntarily. He was bald. He didn't look like any of our composites."

By the time the task force formed in fall 2006, Amherst had assembled reams of paper on the Bike Path Rapist. It was only natural, he suggested, that Sanchez's name be buried somewhere in those files. In fact, Josh

Keats had warned the Amherst officers to be ready for that revelation when the case broke.

"It was nice to get that one done before I retired," Monan concluded.

Between 2007 and 2008, the district attorney's office was rocked by change in the wake of the Bike Path Rapist and other high-profile cases. Ken Case, the veteran prosecutor who worked with the task force, resigned from his job. The following winter, he declared candidacy for the District Attorney's office, hoping to unseat his former boss, Frank Clark, in the Democratic primary. Clark, however, announced in May 2008 that he would not seek re-election due to health issues.[32] Observers theorize that his battles with Delano and other law enforcement officers eroded the public's trust in his leadership, and perhaps were at least part of the reason for his retirement. After much back-room maneuvering, deputy district attorney Frank Sedita, who prosecuted Sanchez, announced his own plans to seek the Democratic endorsement for the top job.

In April 2008, near the one-year anniversary of his exoneration, Anthony Capozzi filed a $41 million lawsuit against New York State. The sum would compensate Capozzi for wages lost during his imprisonment. It would also cover future medical costs.

After his release, Capozzi spent time at the Buffalo Psychiatric Center before moving to an assisted living facility. He spends a few days each week with his family. His impact continues to resonate. In the summer of

---

[32] Clark suffers from lupus, a disease that attacks the immune system.

2007, Governor Eliot Spitzer signed a resolution that streamlined the process for wrongly convicted inmates to seek restitution from the state. The measure was nicknamed "Anthony's Law." A year later, in honor of his plight, a street corner near the family home was christened "Anthony Capozzi Way."

As Scott Patronik reflected on how the case impacted careers, he considered why this investigation was successful after years in which a killer eluded capture.

"We realized the strength of multi-agency cooperation," he cited. "It boils down to different groups working together. If Buffalo police weren't involved, for example, Majane Mazur might have been considered just another homicide. The information needed to catch Sanchez was already in place, but it was scattered among different agencies. We had to come together to solve it."

Patronik is quick to credit previous generations of officers, particularly police who investigated assaults in the 1980s and '90s. Because of their paper trail, he was able to break the case by tracing Wilfredo Caraballo, who owned the car in which Sanchez was spotted days after a 1981 rape.

"I don't even know many of the officers who filed reports," Patronik admitted. "But we stood on their shoulders. Without their hard work years ago, this case wouldn't have been solved."

Altemio Sanchez will remain incarcerated for the rest of his days. Since the sentencing in August 2007, his name occasionally trickles into the news cycle. That fall, someone close to the investigation leaked a phone call with his wife that was recorded while he was in the Erie County Holding Center. The tape was played as part of a TV news segment that did not contain new information, but simply summarized the case.

In October 2007, Kathleen was granted a divorce, and she continued to publicly disavow Sanchez's actions. She told friends she had severed all contact with her ex-husband. Yet well-placed sources confirm that she maintained regular phone conversations with him at Clinton Correctional Facility, as recently as May 2008. The scope of their relationship and the fact that it appears ongoing remains puzzling to those who investigated Sanchez's crimes.

"I take Mrs. Sanchez at her word that she didn't know what he was doing," reflected Amherst detective lieutenant Joseph LaCorte. "But personally, I wonder why is she still supporting him? He admitted he did it."

While Sanchez has faded from the news, visitors to the jail often seek an audience with him. Reporters vying for an inside scoop on the serial killer's behavior are usually turned away. Investigators from outside the task force travel across the state for the opportunity to interview him, trying to link Sanchez to unsolved rapes and murders in their villages. Although he has spoken to them, little new information has been unearthed.

"I don't believe we will ever know all the rapes that this guy committed," Savage reflected. "To him, raping a girl was like a night on the town. I believe he started back in 1977, when he was a senior in high school. The first one we can prove was in 1981. During the four years in between, there were probably a dozen more that were never connected through DNA. For as many as we know about, there are probably an equal number that were never reported."

On Sunday, June 8, 2008, *Dateline NBC* aired a two-hour episode dealing with Western New York's high-profile cold cases. The first hour repeated a broadcast from the prior September about Sanchez and the Bike Path rapes, while the second half focused on Crystallynn Girard's murder. Nearly eight million people watched nationwide.

At Clinton Correctional Facility, the TV provided background to inmates' lives. In the APP Unit, where Sanchez is housed among 250 others, prisoners sat up and took notice when video of their fellow prisoner flashed across the screen.

"That's Al," one of them said.

Everyone's attention turned to the television. They watched as Sanchez was described as a good neighbor, a regular guy who lived a quiet, middle-class life. He held a factory job and worked the night shift. He was married, attended church, and coached Little League baseball. Some kids even called him "Uncle Al."

This contrasted with the image of him given by Erie County sheriff Timothy Howard, recorded in January 2007, stepping before a microphone. Appearing crisp and somber in his black uniform, he told reporters, "The monster that's known as the Bike Path Rapist has been taken into custody."

Few inmates at Clinton knew about Sanchez's crimes. Some from Western New York recognized his name, but part of the prison code is that convicts do not talk about their reasons for being behind bars. A snitch may be listening, and words can be twisted or manipulated.

Thanks to *Dateline NBC*, everyone in the unit suddenly knew what Sanchez had done.

"He's a fucking rapist?" one man asked rhetorically. A buzz traveled throughout the room. Within the prison hierarchy, child molesters and rapists are often targeted for attacks. As Sanchez earned national TV attention for raping and killing women, anger percolated and threatening talk began to escalate.

The next day Sanchez complained about his fate. He was now a marked man, unsafe anywhere except within the confines of his solitary cell. Going to the yard for free time, which had been the only break in his monotony of days, was suddenly an unwise idea. He needed to take extra precautions and be aware of everyone around him.

"Why do they have to keep showing that on TV?" he lamented.

People Who Were Interviewed

Dennis Delano
Alan Rozansky
Greg Savage
Scott Patronik
Lissa Redmond
Josh Keats
Ed Monan
Joseph LaCorte
Ken Case
Pam Guenther
Albert Capozzi Sr.
Mary Capozzi
Ryan Garra
Janine Drmacich
Frank Conway
Michael Sauer

Acknowledgments

Thank you to Paul Randall, Tom Best, Kerri O'Donnell, Ross Brewitt, Stuart Shapiro, Tim O'Shei, Meredith Davis, Joshua L. Rosenberg, Cheryl Delano, Jennifer Noble-Dunlap, Wynne Everett, Colin Conway, Penny Stekl, Kevin and Marcia Mugridge, Marcia McCarthy, and Tom and Mary Jo Schober.

—Jeff Schober

I want to thank Jeff Schober for his friendship and support, and for all of the hours he spent in silence while I ranted about the injustice, inhumanity, and plain disrespect that human beings display for one another. Also for seeing the need to write an honest "all bases covered" account of the investigation of these crimes. It has been a pleasure to work with him.

I reiterate that I played but a small part in the Bike Path Rapist investigations, and that there were people that worked harder and accomplished much more than I did during the investigations of these cases. If not for the meticulous documentation, old-fashioned police work and preservation of old files by past investigators, these cases would still be ongoing and my friend Anthony would still be in custody, because it was by searching backward that we were able to move these cases forward to a successful resolution.

Thanks goes out to New York State Police Captain Steve Nigrelli for his leadership and guidance during this difficult investigation, as well as every investigator from the various departments that worked on the task force and caused all of the pieces of the puzzle to fall into place in a short time frame.

My special admiration and thanks to my colleague, detective Lissa Redmond, for her diligence, tenacity, and commitment to "doing the right thing" that made all this craziness bearable and kept us focused on the task at hand. I apologize for any "collateral damage" incurred on my behalf.

I would also like to thank my "buds" from the Erie County Sheriffs Office, who evolved into great homicide investigators and stood up with me when everyone else was running the other way. I would be remiss if I did not mention Lieutenant Ron Kenyon, who took charge early on. Thank you to Sheriff Timothy Howard for having the leadership and common sense to put this group together and for lending us Chief Scott Patronik. Without him the task force would have imploded on itself and accomplished nothing. I am honored to call him my friend.

Special thanks to my children and grandchildren for understanding that I could only be in one place at a time and that sometimes others have to come first.

I thank God for having had the opportunity to meet and help such a wonderful family as the Capozzis in some small way, and to have been able to play a part in obtaining long-awaited justice for their son and brother. I take great pleasure in calling them my "other family."

Most of all I want to thank my wife Cheryl for sticking by me, for putting up with the unusual life of a police officer, for enduring the long hours and nights spent reviewing paperwork, statements and cases at home, as well as the help and encouragement she selflessly gave to overcome any obstacle that was put my path during this overwhelming investigation. After 38 years, I still love you lots.

—Dennis Delano

About the Authors

Jeff Schober is a graduate of Bowling Green State University and the University at Buffalo. He is the author of *Undercurrent*, a novel set in Western New York, and a co-author of *Sabres: 26 Seasons in Buffalo's Memorial Auditorium*. He has written for a variety of publications, on topics ranging from sports to politics to book reviews. He has acted in Shakespeare plays in Southern Ontario and works as a high school teacher.

With more than twenty years as an investigator for the Buffalo police, Detective Dennis Delano joined the city's newly formed Homicide/Cold Case Squad in 2006. After a successful conclusion to the Bike Path Rapist case, Delano uncovered another instance of wrongful imprisonment. As details emerged about Lynn DeJac's plight, Delano was suspended for releasing information to the media.

Index